DANIEL P. MANNIX

THE HELLFIRE CLUB

AVAILABLE NOW

THE HELLFIRE CLUB

DANIEL P. MANNIX

ibooks
new york
www.ibooksinc.com

DISTRIBUTED BY SIMON & SCHUSTER, INC

An Original Publication of ibooks, inc.

An ibooks, inc. Book

ibooks, inc.
24 West 25th Street
New York, NY 10010

The ibooks World Wide Web Site Address is:
http://www.ibooksinc.com

You can visit the ibooks Web site for a free read and
download the first chapters of all the ibooks titles:
http://www.ibooksinc.com

ISBN 0-7434-1315-6
First ibooks printing May 2001
10 9 8 7 6 5 4 3 2 1

Cover design by Mike Rivilis
Interior design by Michael Mendelsohn and MM Design 2000

Printed in the U.S.A.

1 Weird stories were told of the fabulously rich and brilliant Sir Francis Dashwood. He'd had a vast system of caves dug in a cliff near his estate at West Wycombe, some 33 miles northwest of London, and villagers passing the entrance late at night told of seeing strange figures dressed in red robes dragging screaming girls into the black entrance. But no one liked to complain, because Sir Francis was such a pleasant gentleman. For example, to celebrate the opening of a new, formal garden on his estate, Sir Francis asked the local minister to arrange a Sunday school picnic on the grounds. The minister was only too happy to oblige and he and Sir Francis watched benignly while the children rollicked over the new garden. The garden was laid out in rather a curious fashion. Near one end were two little mounds, each surmounted by a bed of bright red flowers, and in the lower section was a triangle of dense shrubbery.

"Ah, but you must see the garden as a whole," Sir Francis explained to the puzzled minister. "I'll take you to the top of a tower so you can look down on it from a height."

The clergyman cheerfully agreed and followed Sir Francis to the top of the tower. He had just time to realize that he was gazing down at a garden elaborately designed to represent the body of a naked woman when Sir Francis gave a signal. Instantly a stream of water gushed from the shrubbery triangle while two fountains concealed in the flowerbeds shot streams of milky water into the air. The minister fainted and had to be revived by Sir Francis's favorite drink—brandy laced with sulphur, or brimstone, as it was called.

As John Wilkes, an intimate of the amazing Sir Francis, later remarked, "Tis astonishing the lengths Francis will go simply to be nasty."

However, "Hell-Fire Francis" was far more than an enormously rich man with a genius for obscenity. He was one of the most influential figures of the 18th Century. He created the notorious Hell-Fire Club, an association dedicated to Black Magic, sexual orgies, and political conspiracies. The club included among its members the Prime Minister of England, the Chancellor of the Exchequer, the Lord Mayor of

London, the First Lord of the Admiralty, the son of the Archbishop of Canterbury, several of England's greatest artists and poets, the Prince of Wales, and even Benjamin Franklin. The American Revolution has been attributed the indirect product of this uncanny group.

The originator and guiding spirit of the club was Sir Francis Dashwood, baronet, heir to one of the great fortunes of the time, and George III's intimate friend. Sir Francis was born in 1708. His father (the first baronet) was a fiercely ruthless man. A wealthy merchant, he had been determined to obtain a title, and after his first wife died he finally succeeded in 1707 by marrying the daughter of the Earl of Westmoreland. The earl's daughter gave birth to Francis shortly before she succumbed to her husband's brutal treatment. The grim old ex-merchant married two more wives before he himself died in 1724, leaving Francis the estate.

The sixteen-year-old boy celebrated his independence by locking himself up in the cellar for a week with a hogshead of claret. He then set out to enjoy the delights of fashionable London society. His guide, philosopher, and friend at this time was the Honourable Jack Spencer, grandson of the Duchess of Marlborough, a well-known rake who had seduced a twelve-year-old flower girl named Fanny Murray on the steps of Covent Garden Theater. Jack's fame did not come from having seduced a child—that was a routine procedure with all the rakes of the period—but because Fanny later became one of the leading courtesans of the day. She was the mistress of Beau Nash, Lord Sandwich, and Sir William Stanhope (the younger brother of the Earl of Chesterfield). Fanny always gave Jack Spencer credit for having started her on her successful career.

Some rough idea of Jack's morals can be gained from a letter given him by Edmund Easy, the keeper of an accomplished prostitute named Molly. Here is the letter:

"Dear Molly,

"On sight thereof permit the Bearer to immediately enter a pair of sheets with you and let him have ingress, egress and regress to your person in such manner as to him shall seem meet for the space of twenty-four hours and no longer and place it to the account of your kind and confident keeper.

Signed Edmund Easy"

Through Jack Spencer, Sir Francis was introduced to London club life. There were many clubs in London at that time. There were the Mohawks who specialized in "tipping the lion"—crushing the noses of people whom they met on the streets and gouging out their eyes. The Mohawks even carried a special iron instrument about with them for distending the mouths of their victims and slitting their cheeks. There were the Blasters who showed themselves naked to passing girls. There were the Mollies who dressed as women and sang to each other "Tell me, gentle hobble-dehoy, art thou girl or art thou boy?" The She-Romps Club dragged passing girls into their club and made them walk on their hands so their skirts would fall over their heads. Then the club members beat them with riding whips on the exposed parts. The Sweaters used to draw their swords and surround some passer-by who was then ordered "not to turn his back on a gentleman." Any gentleman standing behind the victim was entitled to prick him in the seat of the pants. When the man whirled around, he presented his back to another gentleman who promptly stabbed him for such rudeness, thus keeping him in a constant sweat. Then there were the Hectors, who specialized in sheer vandalism. The members wandered the streets at night ripping knockers off doors, smashing windows, and tearing down shutters. After one of their evening frolics, the leader boasted that "there isn't a window left unbroken on Chancery Lane." The Fun Club went in for practical jokes. Their most famous exploit was to set fire to a line of workmen's cottages and watch the inmates escaping in their nightclothes. The young lord who thought up this joke was crowned "King of Fun."

The members of these clubs were all wealthy young noblemen and so were virtually immune from arrest. However, occasionally they ran into a little trouble. Lord Charteris, who was president of the Man-Killers, tried to nail a night watchman in his sentry box—one of the cylindrical, pillar-like boxes in which the watchmen took shelter during rainy weather. This stunt was called "boxing the watch" and once the man was nailed inside, the box was turned over on its side and rolled down a hill. Although Lord Charteris had two pals to help him, the watchman drew his sword and captured all three Man-Killers. He marched them to the nearest police station, where the judge fined the noblemen 3/4d each (about $1.50) and reprimanded the watchman for interfering with the fun of the nobility. It must be admitted that on a few occasions, the antics of the clubmen got a little out of hand. In 1720, two young aristocrats riding in sedan chairs met at a narrow intersection, and the chair men got into an argument as to who was to give way to the other. The noblemen piled out of their chairs and joined in the dispute. The chair men started fighting with their fists and the young lords with their swords. Other gentlemen rushed out of the coffee houses and joined in the fight. The London mob, always ready for some excitement, promptly took sides. The result was a riot so serious that the Horse Guards had to be called out to break up the crowd with their sabers.

All the clubs specialized in sex. On the bulletin boards were posted lists of famous madams and noted prostitutes, with their specialties listed after each girl's name, somewhat like the batting average of well-known ball players. The madams usually were given picturesque names. Mother Sulphur, her face painted black, led a masked line of naked men and girls through the halls of the Sheet-Lightning Club, and Mrs. Brimstone specialized in providing virgins, all under fifteen, to club members. At the same time, the clubs had a curiously adolescent attitude towards sex that sounds more like a modern college fraternity than a group of dissolute hell rakes. They seemed to have enjoyed boasting about their amatory exploits more than performing them, held endless "bull sessions" on the art of seduction, and exchanged secret lists of young ladies of fashion who could be made. The whole business followed strict rules. If you wanted to seduce a lady, you first sent her reams of poetry full of obscure classical allusions and then, instead of telling her to meet you at the Red Lion Inn where you could register as Mr. and Mrs. Jones, you hid under her bed or climbed in her window at midnight disguised as an Indian rajah. It had to be romantic. It was understood by both sides that you'd afterwards boast of your conquest in every coffee house you frequented in London.

At the age of twenty-one, Sir Francis departed with a tutor for the continent of Europe to make the Grand Tour. The Grand Tour was then considered a necessity for a young gentleman of title, but Sir Francis managed to add a few details not generally included in the itinerary. In the words of his distracted tutor, "He fornicated his way across Europe." Possibly his most outstanding feat was to seduce the

Empress Anne of Russia while disguised as Charles XII of Sweden. Sir Francis turned up at the Russian court elaborately tricked out as King Charles, and speaking a sort of gibberish which he claimed was Swedish. As the real Charles XII had died earlier, it's hard to believe that the Empress was honestly fooled by the young lord, but Anne was fond of dashing men, especially if they had the reputation of being experts in bed. According to all accounts, she went along with the gag. The story is an interesting example of how Sir Francis, even as a young man, loved make-believe. This passion for playing a romantic role stayed with him all his life.

After leaving Russia, Sir Francis and his tutor went on to Turkey, where Sir Francis exhibited "the staying powers of a stallion and the impetuosity of a bull," as Horace Walpole later remarked. Sir Francis dressed in Turkish robes, wore a jeweled scimitar, and sat on a heap of cushions smoking a hookah while beautiful girls (hired for the occasion) nude to the waist and wearing transparent gossamer trousers, paraded before him. At intervals, Sir Francis would remove the mouthpiece of the hookah long enough to exclaim "By the Prophet's Beard, 'tis indeed a houri from Paradise!" or some other Oriental remark, until he'd made his choice for the evening.

After leaving Turkey, Sir Francis and his long-suffering tutor went to Italy. Italy proved to be the climax of the

Grand Tour, and the events there set the pattern for the rest of Sir Francis' life.

To an Englishman with artistic tastes, Italy was an enchanted country. Sir Francis was more than simply a young man dedicated to wine and women; he was also one of the outstanding connoisseurs of art and literature of his age. He could become intoxicated with the great, rolling lines of Virgil as easily as on claret, and the sweeping lines of a vase fascinated him as much as the swinging buttocks of a pretty girl. He'd had little chance to indulge his artistic craving in England of the period, but in Italy he swam in beauty. As though trying to make up for a lifetime of neglect, he feverishly bought statuary, the works of the ancient Greek and Latin poets, and *objets d'art*, never worrying about price and never accepting anything but the best. Even greater than his craving for beauty was his passion for the exotic quality of the past. He spent days wandering through catacombs whose walls were lined with shelves containing the half-mummified corpses of men and women dead two thousand years. He sat by moonlight in the ruins of Roman villas, trying to summon up a vision of the wild orgies which the pale marble walls had once witnessed. He spent days wandering through twisting alleys, feeling well rewarded if he stumbled on some crumbling Roman temple, a half-deserted medieval chapel or an obscure taproom where the proprietor was able to arrange some unusual form of vice for the benefit of a wealthy young English tourist.

Most of all, Sir Francis was interested in the Roman Catholic Church. Since the Revolution in 1688, when James II, the last Catholic monarch, had been driven out of England, Catholicism had been under a cloud in Great Britain, and to young men like Sir Francis it had become surrounded by an aura of horrified fascination. Like many people of his time, the young man had a desperate need for religion— especially a religion with the magnificent pomp and ceremony of Catholicism. The Church of England had become both highly stylized and politically dominated. Many of the clergy were hopelessly corrupt, and the church services were dull and uninspired. Thackeray wrote "[At this time] the stately old English High Church was emptying itself." Yet as an ardent follower of the sceptical Voltaire and the cynical Rabelais, Sir Francis felt duty-bound to sneer at all religion. Still, he haunted the cathedrals with the desperation of a dehydrated man trying to reach a fountain even though it may prove to be a mirage.

As a result of this schizophrenic frame of mind, Sir Francis while in Rome indulged in a prank that not only stamped him for life but also may have changed the history of the world.

The young lord and his tutor had been making a tour of the churches in Rome, Sir Francis alternating between raucous contempt and a tearful yearning for the soul-satisfying faith he saw about him. His tutor, who was an ardent Catholic, was torn between horror at his charge's insulting behavior at the world-famous shrines and pity for the youth who a few minutes later would kneel sobbing at the altar rails, begging God to give him some sign so he could believe. The tour ended at the tiny but exquisite Sistine Chapel. Although it was late in the evening, the chapel was crowded with worshippers holding lighted candles as they knelt at their devotions. Directly behind the altar and covering the entire south wall of the chapel is Michelangelo's great and terrible fresco of the Last Judgment. For the first time the impressionable young Sir Francis saw this famous painting depicting the dead rising from their graves while gloating fiends with scourges drive the wicked to the flames of everlasting hell. In the congregation, penitents flogged themselves with small, symbolic scourges, while keeping up the ancient cry of *"Mea culpa!"*

Kneeling at the back of the chapel, Sir Francis was possessed by the noble murals, the magic of the semidark chapel, and the strange ecstasy of the worshippers. When the service was over, he and his tutor headed for the nearest tavern to drink themselves virtually insensible before going to bed, as was their usual custom. A few bottles of Chianti later, Sir Francis suddenly began to roar with laughter.

"If these Papists are sincere in their penitence, I know how to test them," he announced. "What a jest! Oh, what a priceless jest to tell the lads at White's and Angelo's when we return to London."

The apprehensive tutor asked him what he had in mind, but Sir Francis refused to say. The young lord retired to bed still going into gales of laughter whenever he thought of his plans for the next day.

The following evening, Sir Francis returned to the chapel wearing a cape which he kept closely wrapped around him. When amidst the singing of solemn hymns the penitents began their symbolic scourging, Sir Francis suddenly produced an enormous horse whip from under his cape and fell on the congregation, lashing madly left and right.

"You wish to do penitence?" he shouted. "Good, I'll give you penitence! Take that . . . and that . . . and that!"

In the semidarkness of the chapel, the wild figure wrapped in a flowing cape seemed to be supernatural. A terrified cry of *"Il Diavolo!"* went up as the congregation tried to escape. Men fought their way through the crowd and women screamed as they were knocked down, while Sir Francis, yelling like a madman, laid about him with the whip. At last the congregation realized that they were dealing with a human being, not a fiend risen from the pit. Sir Francis was thrown out of the chapel, still wildly flourishing his whip and yelling obscenities.

"What a jest!" howled the young man to his terrified tutor. "Come, man, we must celebrate!" The tutor needed a drink as much as Sir Francis and they repaired to the nearest tavern. Sir Francis, wild with excitement, started on one of his historic drinking bouts. The tutor gave up early in the evening, but his charge kept on and on. At intervals, Sir Francis would hurl an empty bottle against the wall and stagger out into the dark streets with the anxious tutor trying vainly to hold him back. The young lord would reel into the nearest church and, rushing up to the altar, lash at the images of the saints with his whip, screaming curses. Then he would stagger out of the church and into the next tavern. "Why heaven did not strike us dead for such blasphemy or why we were not knifed by some furious Lazzaroni, I cannot imagine," the tutor later wrote. Probably it was so late at night that few people were in the churches and those were too astonished at what they saw to take action.

The tutor finally managed to lead Sir Francis back to the inn where they were staying, and the baronet passed out cold on his bed. The tutor went to bed in his own room, glad the adventures of the night were at last over. But a few hours later he was awakened by a series of the most blood-curdling shrieks from his charge's room. The tutor recognized Sir Francis' voice screaming for help, but mingled with the human voice were cries like the lost souls of hell coming to seize their prey. The tutor sprang out of bed and still in his nightgown, rushed into the room.

Sir Francis was crouched on the bed, frantic with terror, and even the tutor staggered back in momentary alarm at the sight that met his eyes. Just below the open window shone four green eyes and from this apparition was coming unearthly wails. Then the tutor recovered himself and approached the window. He saw at once that the eyes belonged to two cats, coupled in sexual union, and the female not liking the business particularly was screaming her head off. The tutor shooed the cats back through the window and then turned to his charge, but Sir Francis was in such a state of fright that nothing could be done with him. The tutor returned to his own room, dressed, and then went back to see how the baronet was coming along. As he entered, the young man sprang from his bed and threw himself at the tutor's feet.

"What an experience I've been through!" he gasped. "A devil with four shining eyes came to carry me to hell for my conduct in the Sistine Chapel. You should have heard his cries of glee as he prepared to fasten his talons on me! But at this moment an angel appeared in a white robe. He drove the devil out of the window and then, after giving me his blessing, vanished. My dear friend, I am converted! I'll spend the rest of my life trying to make amends for my evil ways and telling all who will listen of this wondrous miracle that has been vouchsafed me."

Here the tutor made a serious mistake. He should have told the hysterical young man what had really happened. Instead, he saw an opportunity to win an important convert to the Catholic faith as well as to save the young baronet from a life of dissipation. He assured Sir Francis that he must have seen a genuine miracle and that the best course for him to follow was to embrace the True Faith and use his great fortune for the good of the church.

Sir Francis plunged into religion with all the enthusiasm he had shown for sex, drink, art, and archeology. He rushed about Rome, describing his wonderful visitation to anyone who would listen. Unfortunately, after his escapade in the Sistine Chapel the police had determined that this young man, lord or not, would have to leave the country. So, in spite of Sir Francis' pleas that he was now a changed man, he and his tutor were put on board a ship bound for England and told not to return.

During the voyage, Sir Francis' enthusiasm for his newly found faith continued. He prayed constantly. He made plans for building a Catholic cathedral in the heart of London. He was determined to convert the royal family; or if they refused to be converted, then he would join the Jacobins and put Bonnie Prince Charlie on the throne. By the time they reached Portsmouth, the tutor would have been willing to settle for the young rake who flogged the congregation in the Sistine Chapel.

In England, Sir Francis continued his frenzied campaign to convert everyone to Catholicism. He engaged architects to build the cathedral and attended mass twice a day. He was never seen without a rosary. He would burst unexpectedly into the coffee shops and start preaching to his astonished friends, who could not understand what had happened to Sir Francis Dashwood, the notorious hell-rake.

The tutor preserved a decorous silence about their Italian adventures, but one evening a group of young dandies decided to find out what had really happened in Rome. They plied the tutor with wine until, half drunk, he finally told them the truth. He thought it a great joke. So did the young men-about-town.

Next morning, the story was repeated in every coffee house. The circumstances of Sir Francis' conversion became the joke of London society. The baronet was not merely humiliated; he suffered a shock from which he never completely recovered. His conviction that he had been singled out by heaven as the standard bearer in a great cause had been sincere. Now he underwent a reaction as violent as had been his conversion. He determined to prove to the world that he was no sentimental dupe. He would devote the rest of his life to ridiculing religion, particularly Catholicism. And not only religion but all moral principles as well.

Sir Francis decided to found a club to further his aims. Not an association of crude hooligans like the Hectors, Mohawks, or Man-Killers, but a club that would attract the best and brightest minds in England. Because the 18th Century was what it was and Sir Francis was what he was, the main emphasis of the club was to be on sex and drink . . . sex and drink of the most involved and esoteric kind. Secondly, the club was to be an organization intended to ridicule religion. Lastly, the club was to be a secret group directing the fate of the nation—a sort of invisible empire operating behind the scenes of government.

That Sir Francis should have succeeded in all of his purposes through an organization that became known as the Hell-Fire Club is a curious commentary on the 18th Century mind. The 18th Century was an era of insecurity. The concept of democracy was fighting against the concept of tyranny. Religion had ceased to make any appeal to many intellectuals. Great Britain had gained control over nearly one-third of the world's surface, but parliament had no idea how to deal with American colonists, Indian princes, and African tribal kings. The threat of a gigantic international conflict (which later actually occurred in the form of the terrible Napoleonic wars) colored everyone's thinking. Young men responded to the confusion around them by forming "gangs" with melodramatic names and committing acts of senseless violence. However, these young men were enormously wealthy and had the education and taste to hit on all kinds of refinements of sex and sadism.

Dickens has called it "the best of times and the worst of times." There were fantastic fortunes. Living was so cheap that Swift's mistress, Stella, could live in "genteel comfort" on an income of £150 a year, yet Lord Durham remarked that a gentleman of fashion "could barely manage to jog along on 40,000 pounds a year." Johnson himself told Boswell, "A man can manage to exist on 6 pounds a year and live comfortably on 30 pounds." While the Prince Regent could spend nearly a million pounds building his Turkish Pavilion as a summer resort at Brighton, taverns in Whitechapel carried signs: "Drunk for a Penny! Dead drunk for two pence! Clean straw to lie on provided free!" In the Lady Guinea gambling house, the lowest stake allowed on the table was fifty guineas and there was never less than 20,000 guineas in the pot. The members wore leather sleeves to save their lace cuffs, leather bibs to protect their ruffles, and nightcaps to hold their curls in order. There was a special dueling room where, in case of a dispute over the cards or dice, the members could retire. Pistols and swords were provided by the management. Although most of London was a casbah of filthy alleys and tunnel-like cellars where millions of men, women, and children lived like rats, the most famous of the "stately homes" of England were built during this period; a few of them still preserved today (including the great mansion built by Sir Francis Dashwood) by the National Trust as tourist attractions.

The 18th Century was an era when "great men were as common as gooseberries." In literature, there were Dr. Johnson, Oliver Goldsmith, Richard Brinsley Sheridan, and the others of the Cheshire Cheese group. Lawrence Sterne was writing *Tristram Shandy*, Jonathan Swift had published *Gulliver's Travels*, and Lord Chesterfield was in the midst of his famous letters to his illegitimate son. In art, Sir Joshua Reynolds, Gainsborough, Sir Thomas Lawrence, George Romney and Hogarth were prominent. In architecture, Sir Christopher Wren had completed St. Paul's, Robert Adams had succeeded Sir John Vanbrugh as the leading architect of "stately homes" and "Capability" Brown did the gardens. A young cabinet maker named Chippendale was beginning to attract attention, as was Hepplewhite. An obscure ensign named Horatio Nelson was amusing himself trying to shoot polar bears, and a sawed-off little Corsican named Napoleon was entering artillery school in France. (His fellow cadets called him "Puss-in-Boots" because he wore high-heeled boots to make himself look bigger.) In the American Colonies, a young surveyor named George Washington was starting on his career, and Benjamin Franklin was already famous in Philadelphia as the author and publisher of *Poor Richard's Almanac.*

None of these minor events meant much to the young bloods of London society. They were far more interested in the Duke of Queensberry, who had hired the three most famous courtesans in London to appear before him nude while he awarded a golden apple to the most beautiful. There was also the intriguing question as to whether the notorious Chevalier d'Eon, the internationally known duelist, was a man or a woman. The Chevalier dressed as both on occasions and had affairs with members of both sexes. Then there was the interesting experiment conducted by Thomas Day, author of the famous boy's book *Sandford and Merton*, who decided to raise a wife to suit himself and got an eleven-year-old girl from an orphan asylum. After training her for three years, he tested her ability to stand pain by pouring hot sealing-wax on her neck and was disappointed when she screamed with agony. Then he fired his pistol between her legs. When the girl yelled, Mr. Day sent her back to the asylum in disgust. Another important figure was Lord Petersham, who ordered his valet to put half a dozen bottles of sherry by his bed and call him the day after to-morrow. Then there was Sir Charles Busbury, who never walked across the floor of a room; he always climbed around on top of the furniture. Horace Walpole caused a sensation by having himself and his mistress buried up to their necks and then employing a hairdresser to do their hair. The Duke of Norfolk could be washed only when he was dead drunk, and Beau Nash rode through the town naked on the back of a cow. These men were the heroes of the young bucks who admiringly discussed and imitated their eccentricities.

Gentlemen of fashion wore high red heels, patted blue

powder on their faces and carried muffs. Their hair was carefully dressed in thirty-six curls, their clothes were covered with fine lace, and tying one's cravat was a long drawn-out ceremony. The women dressed even more elaborately. No lady of fashion appeared before three o'clock in the afternoon; it took her that long to get her clothes on, with the help of several maids. Both men and women "received" in bed during the mornings: the men were surrounded by a horde of jockeys, tailors, hairdressers, gamblers, and dancing masters; the women by jewelers, dressmakers, cosmetic experts, milliners, and music teachers. Entering a room was an art. A gentleman came in on tiptoes "as though the floor were wet and he were afraid of falling," with his hat clasped to the pit of his stomach. He then placed the hat under one arm, advanced one foot, bowed at a perfect 90-degree angle, and remained in that position until recognized.

The ladies had even a harder time. Their headdresses were nearly a yard high, composed of two or three stories of wire frames covered with tiffany and artificial hair. The Duchess of Devonshire stuck two ostrich feathers in her hairdo, each feather over a yard long, thus starting a new fashion which added to the general complications. Hoopskirts were often eight feet in diameter, and six or seven petticoats were worn underneath. All the gentlemen took snuff, and the boxes were exquisite in design and made of the most expensive materials. A gentleman had to be able to open his box in the act of extending it by raising the lid between his thumb and first finger. There were "snuff masters" who did nothing but teach young bucks the art of taking snuff.

The bucks were not cowards. Dueling was as routine as love-making. The father of Laurence Sterne fought a duel with a Captain Philip over a goose. Philip ran his opponent through the body with such force that the captain's sword stuck in the wall behind Mr. Sterne. Mr. Sterne politely asked the captain if he'd mind wiping the plaster off the point of his sword before withdrawing it. Two fashionably dressed gentlemen engaged in a duel with pistols and as the shots rang out, one man uttered a scream of mortal agony. "A surgeon, a surgeon!" shouted the seconds. "A tailor, a tailor!" screamed the stricken duelist. "His bullet has ruined my new coat!" Duels were fought in the coffee houses, in the streets, in Hyde Park, and in the parlors of fashionable homes. For a buck to admit that he hadn't killed his man was as deep a disgrace as admitting to being a virgin.

Even when the rakes walked the streets they were followed by retinues of down-and-out artists, sculptors, couriers and foreign travel, purveyors of pornographic literature, wine merchants, and pimps. The noblemen had discovered Europe, art, and pornography, and their interests were about evenly divided among the three. Hard liquor had recently been introduced into society and revolutionized drinking habits. The passion for the macabre was as strong as with our own adolescents. A motion picture such as *I Was a Teenage Werewolf* would have been as popular then as now. To give an eerie quality to their estates, the noblemen planted dead trees on the grounds and hired hermits to live in specially dug caves. They even employed men to tame bats, vipers, and owls to live in the artificial caves with the hermits. In a wild attempt to capture the ghostly grandeur of Italy and Greece, they built ruined temples in out-of-the-way corners of their gardens and got sculptors to make statues with missing heads, arms, and legs, to resemble the antique statues that were so mutilated. The School of Terror appeared in literature, started by Horace Walpole's famous novel *The Castle of Otranto* the original of all the haunted castles in fiction. It was followed by "Monk" Lewis' great work in which a girl is locked in a cellar with the dead body of her illegitimate baby. The mother continues to try to nurse the decaying child and is delighted to find that she is wearing white rings ... maggots are crawling around her fingers. There was such a passion for vampires, ghosts, ghouls, and werewolves that some young men insisted on drinking their wine out of skulls especially stolen for them from the graveyards by body-snatchers.

It was in this atmosphere that Sir Francis set about founding his club. There had been for many years a Hell-

Fire Club which held its meetings at an old inn called George and Vulture on George Yard in London. The proprietor kept a huge vulture as a theatrical prop and this weird touch endeared the place to the rakes. (The inn is still standing, and Dickens laid several scenes in *Pickwick Papers* there.) The original Hell-Fire Club had been abolished by special order of the Lord High Chancellor, because even in that broadminded time the members had carried things a little too far when they celebrated Mass on the body of a naked girl stretched out on one of the barroom tables. But Sir Francis was delighted by the club's principles and set up his own circle at the George and Vulture in imitation of the earlier group.

Sir Francis did not call his association the Hell-Fire Club. In many ways he despised the earlier rakes as a lot of ignorant peasants. But the public considered the new society to be merely a continuation of the old and called it by the same name. The Hell-Fire Club it has remained ever since.

Sir Francis called his group The Friars of St. Francis of Wycombe. There were twelve members, each named after one of the twelve apostles. Sir Francis took the part of Christ. For several months, they met in the cellar of the George and Vulture, but, as the accommodations were limited and the police were apt to interfere with their parties, they moved to an island in the Thames near Hampton Court. Meanwhile, Sir Francis was busily engaged in finding a suitable clubhouse for his group. At last, some time in 1752, he hit on the perfect spot. It was a ruined Medieval abbey located on the bank of the Thames near Marlow, some six miles from Sir Francis' estate at West Wycombe. The abbey was surrounded by a grove of magnificent old elms which almost completely concealed it. A little stream ran by the crumbling walls, and beyond lay open meadows. The nearest highway was several miles away. The setting was so romantic that years later Shelley used to go to the abbey to compose his poems. The members could come up the river in private barges with their girls, spend the night in the abbey, and return by the same route—much simpler than having to ride or coach several miles to an equally secluded spot. In addition, the ruined abbey was exactly the sort of setting Sir Francis needed for his ceremonies. It was weird, isolated, and old, and the chapel was still intact. The chapel was important. The friars—or, as they usually called themselves, "the monks"—needed a consecrated chapel for Black Mass ceremonies.

The abbey was called Medmenham (pronounced "Mednam") and had been built in 1160. It had been long deserted. Sir Francis was able to purchase it with little trouble. He then set about rebuilding it, but rebuilding it still to resemble a ruin. For romantic reasons the abbey must look as though it were ready to collapse at any minute.

The rebuilding was elaborate. The workmen were imported from distant parts of the British Isles, were sworn to secrecy and were kept under constant guard. The chapel was done over according to Sir Francis' tastes. Stained glass windows were installed, which bore pictures of the "twelve apostles" in costume, each in some indecent pose. On the ceiling was painted a magnificent fresco in brilliant colors, also pornographic. Unfortunately, we don't know the subject. People who were admitted into this Holy of Holies merely say it was too terrible to describe. John Wilkes, who heaven knows was no prude, calls it "unspeakable." At the far end of the chapel was a tiny window and directly under it the altar made of black Italian marble. In front of it ran beautifully carved altar rails. Over the door of the chapel was engraved the Latin quotation, "Stranger, refuse, if you can, what we have to offer."

Sir Francis also built a Roman Room whose walls were decorated with copies of the indecent paintings from ancient Roman frescos. Along the sides of the room were arranged richly upholstered couches for the use of the monks and their sweethearts. In niches were statues of Egyptian gods. There were also paintings of famous prostitutes and the kings of England. The portrait of Henry VIII had a strip of paper pasted over the face as punishment because Henry had closed the monasteries. Over the entrance was written in Latin, "Dare to despise convention."

Next to the Roman Room was the library, containing

what was generally admitted to be the finest collection of pornographic books in Great Britain. The library also contained a splendid assortment of religious books. The two collections were all mixed in together—*Fanny Hill* being sandwiched in between *The Book of Common Prayer* and *Sherlock on Death*, while the *Kama Sutra* (a famous Oriental treatise showing the 365 possible positions of sexual intercourse) was bound as *The Reformed Hymnal*. There was also a Robing Room and Withdrawing Room. A series of small private rooms called "cells" were connected to the Withdrawing Room. Each cell was equipped with a couch covered with green silk.

In addition to all this, Sir Francis installed a cellar of fine wines and a larder full of delicacies, and outfitted the abbey with magnificent Gobelin tapestries and the best Chippendale, Adams, and Hepplewhite furniture. Sir Francis had excellent taste.

A small staff of trusted servants was maintained at the abbey to wait on the monks and keep up the place, but only the members themselves were allowed in the chapel. Not even the girls could go there. The chapel was regarded by the monks with great devotion and was a sacred spot which they never entered without due ceremony.

Over the entrance of the abbey was inscribed *"Fay ce que voudras"* ("Do what thou wilt"). The writing was made in imitation of the 17th Century style and was such an accurate forgery that until recently it deceived experts. On one side of the door was a statue of Harpocrates, the Egyptian god of silence, with his finger to his lips, and on the other side a statue of Volupian Angerona (the goddess of secret passion) in the same attitude. There were no clocks in the abbey, so the brothers couldn't mark the passing of time.

The woods around the abbey were filled with statuary, marble pillars engraved with Latin inscriptions, little temples in the Grecian style, and artificially designed "cozy nooks" generally equipped with transplanted beds of soft moss or stone couches covered with fine cushions. The inscriptions were written in what was sarcastically called "macaroni Latin," macaroni being the slang name for an elegant young gentleman ("Yankee Doodle stuck a feather in his hat and called it macaroni"). Macaroni Latin was a sort of bastard language in which the Latin words were twisted to make puns in English or combined in such a way as to create a ridiculous effect. There was a statue of Hermes, who among his other attributes was the god of lust, holding a staff carved as a phallic symbol with the tip painted red. Under it was engraved "Peni Tento non Penitenti" which can be roughly translated as "A penis tense rather than penitence." Over one of the couches was written "A lover dies on the breast of his mistress." Carved on the side of a great oak was the inscription "Here a nymph fled from the arms of a satyr after having been ravished." A nude statue of

Venus bending over to take a thorn from her foot was set up at a sharp bend in a woodland path so that anyone turning the corner would run into the bare buttocks of the goddess. Wilkes wrote, "Just over the two nether hills of snow were these lines: [English translation] 'This is where the path divides . . . between lies the road to Paradise. But to indulge in such perversions condemns one to hell.' " There was even a marble outhouse, beautifully designed, called "The Temple of Cloacina" (the goddess of the sewer or of the intestinal tract). This shrine was also known to the brotherhood as "The Temple of Ease."

Dashwood even went to the lengths of having an artificial cave hollowed out in a little hill, which he called the Cave of Trophonius. In classical lore, Trophonius' Cave was a mysterious grotto "from whence all creatures came out melancholy." This was a pretty elaborate pun, explained by a fresco and Latin inscription over the entrance. The fresco showed a collection of livestock, including a crowing cock and a laughing nun. The inscription read: "All animals after sexual intercourse feel melancholy except the barnyard cock or a priestess, who love to give it away." Inside the cave was a more elaborate inscription on the wall. A very free translation would be: "Sweat and exchange sweat until the marrow of your bones runs out."

These inscriptions give a good idea of the mental capacities of the Friars of St. Francis. The brotherhood was able not only to translate the tortuous Latin-English puns but also to appreciate the allusion to Trophonius' Cave, which implies a considerable classical knowledge. But imagine the cost and trouble involved in having sculptors make such statues and hiring stone-cutters to engrave these inscriptions! English schoolboys still like to scribble pornographic puns in Latin on lavatory walls, but the obscenities at the abbey were the product of some of the most outstanding men of the time. Several contemporary connoisseurs of art who saw the "Garden of Lust" considered it a terrific waste of time, but all agree that the landscaping was beautifully conceived and that the statues were magnificently executed. It was as if a potentially great poet had devoted his time to writing obscene poems rather than composing first class verse—although some obscene poems are very clever.

The arrival of the monks at the abbey must have been an impressive sight. It always took place at night. There was a special large gondola, painted bright red, which belonged to the club and was used to ferry the monks and their girls from London to the abbey, although some of the brotherhood preferred to come in their own boats. After arriving at the landing, the monks donned white robes with hoods lined with scarlet and marched towards the abbey holding lighted tapers. Meanwhile, a bell tolled from the tower of the abbey and ghostly music was played by an organ hidden in a wing.

Boatmen on the river and travelers who had lost their way occasionally witnessed this awesome spectacle. Most of them thought that the spirits of the dead monks were returning to their abbey and promptly fled—which was exactly what the Friars wanted them to do. As the procession approached the abbey the statues of Harpocrates and the Volupian Angerona on either side of the door were illuminated by lanterns hidden in the shrubbery. At the entrance stood Sir Francis, also in a white robe but wearing a Cardinal's red hat. He cried out, "What is the password?"

The monks responded together: "Do what thou wilt!"

The procession then entered the abbey, led by the Abbot of the Day. The monks took turns for this honor. The Abbot arranged the menu, selected the wines, and organized the entertainment for the evening. He also had first pick of the women.

Inside the abbey, the lights burned behind panes of red glass which filled the Roman Room with a subdued, rosy twilight. From a silver chalice, probably engraved with pornographic designs (Hogarth has an engraving showing it, but most of the chalice was decorously covered by cloth), Sir Francis poured brandy laced with brimstone into glasses shaped like horns. A solemn toast was drunk to the powers of darkness. A deep-toned gong was struck and the procession marched into the chapel.

Some time before, Dashwood had obtained a book on

black magic from the bookseller Edmund Curll, who had a publishing house in Covent Gardens where he published pornographic works for a select coterie. Dashwood was one of his best customers. At his patron's request, Curll obtained for him a treatise on occultism, probably a copy of *The Key of Solomon* or the *Kabala*. At that time, books on occultism were illegal and considered in the same class as pornography, and only illicit publishers handled them. This book, whatever it was, was the basis for the club's magical ceremonies.

There are two theories behind Satanism. One is that in view of all the evil there is in the world, Satan is really God and should be worshipped as such, since no merciful God would permit wars, disease, famines, floods, earthquakes, and all the miseries around us. The other theory is that Satan is the natural leader of all rebels who rise against the injustices of king, church, and society. Satan is a heroic figure who refuses to be pushed around. The theologian Martensen claimed that Satan was Christ's younger brother who refused to take second place. Milton reflects this attitude in *Paradise Lost*, when Satan, after being defeated and condemned to eternal punishment, says proudly, "Better to reign in hell than serve in heaven." The monks of St. Francis probably took this position, as they themselves were rebels against convention. At that time, the conception of church and state as one unit, as typified by the "divine right of kings," was so prevalent that to be cynical about one automatically meant being cynical of the other. These men were nearly all closely connected with the government and knew it was a seething mass of corruption. They were on intimate terms with the royal family and knew that the king, George II, was a fool, and that the crown prince, Frederick, was, if anything, even worse. Several members of the club were clergymen and knew that the English High Church was as corrupt as the government. By contrast, Satan seemed a strong, determined figure—gay, imaginative, dashing, and cheerfully immoral. As one writer put it, "They made the Prince of Darkness over in the shape of an 18th Century gentleman."

It's hard to tell how seriously the club took their Satanism; in fact, it's hard to tell how seriously they took anything. It was the fashion to be cynical about love, honor, patriotism, and religion. At the same time, the rakes were capable of fighting to the death for a moral issue, ruining themselves to help others, and even dying of a broken heart over the death of a friend. The Earl of Sandwich, the most notorious rake of the whole lot, who boasted that he specialized in seducing virgins because he enjoyed "the corruption of innocence, for its own sake," went into retirement after the death of one of his innumerable mistresses. Dashwood nearly ruined himself trying to help Benjamin Franklin obtain support for the American colonists. It was a time when the old values were being destroyed and men were desperately trying to find new standards—but always in a sneering, superior fashion.

Although the brothers wrote about their amorous adventures at the abbey in considerable detail, they didn't say much about their celebration of the Black Mass, since that was considered even by 18th Century standards a terrible sin. We do know that the chapel was draped in black and there were missals on exhibition containing obscene parodies of the scriptures, probably along the lines of the Latin inscriptions in the garden. For the rest, the ceremony probably followed the general lines of the traditional Black Mass still occasionally practiced today by screwball groups. The Mass was celebrated on the body of a naked woman laid out on the altar and the congregation drank the sacrificial wine from her navel. The crucifix was inverted and black candles were burned. Lamps of lewd design were used. (One in the shape of a monster bat with an erect penis is still preserved in the Witchcraft Museum on the Isle of Man.) Sir Francis probably conducted the service, although, according to the statement of a contemporary writer who had talked to the monks, the Abbot of the Day had this privilege. This bogus priest seems to have worn a robe fastened with gold buttons on which were engraved the Sign of the Cross and the letters IHS. In braziers around the room magical herbs were burned: belladonna, hemlock, henbane, verbena, and mandrake—all powerful narcotics. The Host was "Holy Ghost Pye," made, according to one authority, from the angelica root, which, from its name, is popularly referred to in England as the Holy Ghost Root. It was a standing joke of the brotherhood to call for a slice of Holy Ghost Pye when in taverns and then exchange knowing winks when the puzzled landlord asked what they meant.

Although except for the bat lamp it is not known what sort of paraphernalia was used, Sir Francis had apparently been able to purchase a large hanging lamp of Rosicrucian design from the proprietor of the George and Vulture. The proprietor had kept this lamp as a novelty, together with his pet vulture, and the Friars had used it to light their meetings in the cellar. The brotherhood would probably have bought the vulture too, but unfortunately it died. The lamp had a design depicting intertwined snakes pursuing doves, and it was seemingly used as a sort of totem by the club. What other occult furnishings were used is not known, but unquestionably they were of the best. Satanists went to great lengths to dress up their altars. King Henry III of France had a Black Mass altar with a section of the True Cross mounted in gold laid into a crucifix with two devils made of solid silver rubbing their behinds on it. Other famous Black Mass services include a silver chalice with a golden devil urinating into the bowl, and a hand-embroidered stole showing victorious demons subjecting the heavenly hosts to obscene humiliations.

The ceremony itself was generally merely a parody of the Catholic Mass; in the case of the Franciscans probably delivered in Macaroni Latin with double meanings. The use of the Mass by magicians was so common that our term "hocus-pocus" derived from *"hic est corpus,"* the words the priest utters when he elevates the Host. The brothers amused themselves writing dirty rhymes set to the tunes of well-known hymns which were sung during the ceremony. A collection of these hymns coming to light years later caused the exile of John Wilkes.

The famous artist William Hogarth was a member of the society and he made a print showing Sir Francis at his devotions. Sir Francis in the habit of a Franciscan monk kneels before a naked woman—probably the goddess whom the brothers call the "Bona Dea." She was also worshipped as Venus, Aphrodite, and Ishtar. Sir Francis is holding a piece of the Holy Ghost Pye, marked with a cross, and with a bite taken out of it. Over "Saint Francis" head is a halo from which peers the grinning, evil face of Lord Sandwich. On the ground beside him lies a split chalice, a rosary, and a missal. This print is in the British Museum.

The usual intent of a Black Mass ceremony is to invoke the devil for magical purposes. The Franciscans probably had no real hope of being able to invoke Satan (although they certainly got a surprise at one of their ceremonies, as will be explained later), and the whole procedure was intended more to ridicule Catholicism than as an actual incantation. In fact, their ceremonies so closely followed the Roman Catholic mass that the monks were denounced by one zealous defender of Protestantism as "devil-worshippers, republicans, sodomists, and Roman Catholics." When an apologist for the club pointed out that the members were merely devil-worshippers and didn't go in for republicanism, sodomy, and Catholicism, the indignant defender of the faith retorted, "Well, if they're devil-worshippers, they must be a kind of Catholic and so they probably do the other things too." The hatred of Catholicism at the time was so intense that this passed as a reasonable argument. The Franciscans did seem to take their Satanism seriously—at least as seriously as modern undergraduates take the oaths and secret rites of their fraternities.

After the chapel ceremony, the brothers entered the Roman Room. Here were waiting a line of girls, dressed as nuns, and masked. Although most of the girls were professional prostitutes, many were the wives and daughters of local merchants and tradesmen who were thrilled at the idea of having a fling with members of the nobility. These women preferred to keep their identity secret. There were even some noted ladies of fashion, but, most surprising of all, a few of the "nuns" were the wives, sisters, or even mothers of the "monks." A contemporary writer said bitterly, "They attempt all females of their own species promiscuously—grandmothers and mothers as well as their own daughters. Even their sisters fear their violence."

There would seem to be some justification for this charge, at least in the case of Sir Francis. He had four half-sisters, daughters of his father's other wives, and there would seem to be good evidence that these girls sometimes attended the parties at the abbey. One of Sir Francis' step-mothers was still alive and she may also have gone, masked, to the orgies. John Hall Stevenson, although not a member of the club, attended some of the meetings and claimed that the former Lady Mary Dashwood did occasionally appear as a "nun" and that Sir Francis enjoyed picking her out of the lineup. The idea of incest fascinated many of the rakes, es-pecially as it bore on the theory of occultism. In magical circles, incestuous relations between a brother and a sister or a father and his daughter were often required. The idea was apparently to bind the members of a family more closely together by forcing them to share a guilt secret so terrible that it would put them beyond the pale of humanity. [The Mau Mau in Kenya also featured obscene rites whose only purpose was to convince the initiate that he was com-pletely divorced from all tribal or religious connections.] I doubt if the Franciscans regarded it as anything more than an exciting way of defying conventions, but like many of their acts it also had a symbolic significance.

John Hall Stevenson wrote a poem about Dashwood's

incestuous relationships. The poem is supposedly written by one of the "nuns" who was picked up as a young girl by a madam supplying the club with virgins. Many of these madams were Lesbians who used the girls themselves before turning them over to men. Some of the references in the poem can no longer be traced. Here's the poem, which is entitled: "The Confessions of Sir F—of Medmenham and of the Lady Mary, his wife":

I was taught at sixteen by a masculine gun
Til I learnt from a pistol to handle a gun,
And then I encountered a friar from Furnes'
That used to serve her and the abbot by turns.

Thus my nun watched the signals and had for her
    pains
Both the abbot's leavings and other small gains,
For the abbot to balance and make accounts fair
Put all the young novices under her care.

Now whether in Sappho 'twas passion or whim
She amused herself better with me than with him,
So we struck up a bargain that pleased us all
    three
And I stuck to the friar and she stuck to me.

Jen played on the flute with her fingers so white
And twinkled her eyes and kept time very right,
Then he served up his cousin, a delicate blade,
And old Bridget his aunt for the sake of her maid.

And lastly, he ravished his lady so meek
When she had not lain-in much more than a
    week,
Although she declared she would give her consent
But had vowed the last week to lie fallow in Lent.

Like a hotspur young cock, he began with his
    mother,
Cheer'd three of his sisters one after the other,
And oft tried little Jen, but gain'd so little ground
Little Jen lost her patience and made him
    compound.

Between friar and knight, my Lesbian's brother,
I was like to become an unfortunate mother,
But by her assistance and skill I miscarried
And at last, through her means, to Sir Francis was
    "married."

"After all," said the Friar, "in all kinds of sport,
A keen sportsman is apt to believe the time's
    short,

So your sins I'll absolve but to wipe them out
  quite
I enjoin you to lie with old Bridget all night."

Sir Francis' wife was not named "Lady Mary," but was Sarah Gould. Sir Francis married her in 1745. She was a highly respectable woman and she and her half-mad husband lived together very happily all their lives. Why Stevenson speaks of "The Lady Mary, his wife," isn't known. One of his stepmothers was called Mary, and this may be a crack at their supposed incestuous relationship, or it may have been one of the nuns who adopted the "magical name" "Lady Mary." Both the monks and the nuns gave themselves elaborate magical names. No one seems to know who "Little Jen" or "Bridget" were. After two hundred years, many references become obscured.

After the Abbot of the Day had made his choice, the other members paired off with the girls. The girls kept on their masks no matter what else they took off, "so that no misunderstanding may arise from an unexpected meeting with one's legal husband or professed admirer." The couples could retire to one of the cells in the Withdrawing Room, wander out into the garden or go to Trophonius' Cave. Apparently most of the couples preferred to remain in the Roman Room and build up their passions by voyeurism (sexual gratification from watching the actions of others). Then monks and nuns undressed each other and after considerable by-play, which often included the recital of magical hymns and incantations, retired to the couches. The communal aspect of the business added to its flavor.

Exhibitionism, as typified by the voyeurism, was for some reason or other a deeply ingrained characteristic of the period. It was the controlling factor in Sir Francis' life and that of many other men. Quite probably it was the result of the feeling of insecurity which overhung the time—the same feeling that today causes a certain type of young man to go in for sideburns, leather jackets, elaborate mannerisms, and endless boastings of his amatory exploits. The Hell-Fire monks with their robes, Black Mass ceremonies, and sexual exhibitionism carried this business to extremes as they did everything else. They couldn't even have sexual relations without an audience. Later, this craving for exhibitionism was to result in the worst riots in the history of London, provoked by a futile young lord in desperate need of recognition.

In John Cleland's famous pornographic work *Fanny Hill*, written in 1749, there are elaborate descriptions of this voyeurism. In the brothels of the period, couches were arranged around the walls for these community exhibitions. Couple after couple would retire to the couches in full view of the others and, after they had finished, watch the others take their turns. The Hell-Fire Club's Roman Room was designed for this purpose. It is interesting that in *Fanny Hill*, the men who insisted on these exhibitions are described as young lords. Ordinary clients preferred privacy. Apparently the aristocracy needed the inspiration of each other's company before they could perform the sexual act.

Most of the "nuns" were recruited from the fashionable bagnios of London. Many of these brothels were as well known as the famous coffee houses such as Almak's, White's, and Boodle's. Some of the more elegant bagnios were Moll King's, Constance Phillips', Lucy Cooper's (who was called "lewder than all the whores of Charles II's reign"), and Elizabeth Roach's. Possibly the most fashionable was Charlotte Hayes' establishment. We know that Charlotte provided some of the Medmenham nuns, for there is a record in her account book: "June 18, 1759. Twelve vestals for the Abbey. Something discreet and Cyprian for the friars."

Sandwich said of Mrs. Hayes, "She keeps the Stock Exchange supplied with real, immaculate maidenheads." Each morning "she took her rounds to see what youth and beauty the country had sent to London. When she found a fresh and pretty rural lass she tricked her up with patch and paint . . . a creature whom she always called a milliner or a parson's daughter."

Some of the extracts from Mrs. Hayes' account book are interesting:

"Jan. 8. A maid for Alderman X. Nell Blossom, about

nineteen, has not been in company these four days and was prepared for a state of vestalship last night.

"Feb. 2. Colonel Y. Wants a modest woman. Mrs. Mitchell's cook-maid being just come from the country and a new face? Or the Countess La Fleur from Seven Dials? If so, her flash-man, La Fleur, must dress her to the best advantage.

"Feb. 17. Dr. Z. After church is over."

From Hogarth's series of etchings called "The Harlot's Progress" and from other sources, we can reconstruct not only the life of these girls but how they were secured. The madams made a business of visiting the inns where young girls who had come to the big city "to make their fortunes" were likely to stay. The madam was an expert at getting information out of a young girl without seeming to ask questions. Usually she offered to buy the girl a glass of wine or some other refreshment. The approach of "Mother Stanhope" ran like this:

"I like to be jolly myself and see others so. I'm getting on now ... ain't what I was once. But as I says I like to be jolly and I always is. An old fiddle, you know, makes the best music."

Sounds like Ma Perkins. After this homey approach, Mother Stanhope would find out if the girl had any friends in London or if her relations in the country were in a position to make trouble. Mother Stanhope always tried to get the name of some distant relation of the girl's. She would then exclaim in astonishment, "Don't tell me that Martha Brown is your aunt! Well, well, I know Martha well . . . although I haven't seen her for a year or two. So you're Martha's niece! Now you must stay at my house while you're in London. I won't charge you a penny and I'll write to Martha that you're with me."

Once in the house, the girl was then offered a job at an excellent salary, generally as a milliner. However, it was necessary for her to sign a contract as an apprentice. As soon as the contract was signed, the girl was then drugged and raped by the establishment's "bully" or what we'd now call the "bouncer." When she recovered, she was told that she was now ruined and could hope for nothing but a career in the bagnio. The contract was produced and in the fine print the girl discovered that she had sworn to put herself completely in the hands of her "protector." Actually, the contract had no legal basis but the terrified country girl had no way of knowing that.

The first house to which the girl was taken was generally "a breaking-in house" or, as Fanny Hill calls it, "a place where the girl was broken to the mounting block." Afterwards she was sent to the regular house. However, in the really de luxe establishments the girl was set up in her own house or at least in an apartment, and the illusion was given that she was a lady of leisure who occasionally received gentlemen visitors. She was given fashionable clothes, a pet monkey, and a little Negro servant boy dressed in Oriental costume, as these props were considered absolutely necessary for a lady of fashion. However, whenever she went out she was always followed by an older woman (generally a retired prostitute) to make sure that the girl didn't sell any of her finery and make enough money to escape.

It may be wondered why the girl didn't cry for help as soon as she got out of the house. Some of the girls who proved difficult were kept as virtual prisoners, but most of them, having lost their virginity and having signed the bogus contract, felt that there was no other course open to them but a life of prostitution. Also, for the first time in her life the girl was well-fed, wore pretty clothes, and was able to meet men of some refinement. The only other work open to most of them was as a servant in some home. Being a servant wasn't a very attractive prospect. For example, here's what happened to a seventeen-year-old girl named Mary Clifford in 1767. Mary had offended her mistress, Elizabeth Brownrigg, and when a neighbor accidentally found the girl tied in an outhouse she looked like this:

"Her head was swelled to almost double the natural size, and her neck so much that she could neither speak nor swallow. Her mouth stood open and the doctor who examined her deposed that she was all one wound from her head to her toes, that her shift stuck to her body, that she was in a fever and the wounds had begun to mortify from neglect."

Most girls were willing to settle for a life of shame.

As long as the girl was being kept by a series of single men, she was comparatively well off, although naturally most of the money she made went to the madam. However, when her charms began to fade, she was put in a house with a number of other girls. Here she was forced to entertain everyone from highwaymen to nobles. Part of her duties were to rob the guests. Hogarth in a painting depicts such a scene. A young rake, two-thirds drunk, sits in a chair while one of the girls steals his watch and passes it over to the madam. Beside the rake are a watchman's staff and lantern, souvenirs of an attack on the watch; much as modern young Englishmen on a drunk feel it necessary to show their valor by coming back with a policeman's helmet. In another part of the room, two girls are having a fight. One spits a mouthful of wine into the other's face and her furious adversary is going for her with a knife. In a corner are a blind harper, a ballad singer who probably specialized in obscene songs, and a trumpeter, all hired for the party. The table is covered with broken wine glasses and overturned bottles. The mirrors are smashed and a roast chicken with a fork stuck in it lies on the floor. This is unquestionably a very accurate picture of the windup of an 18th Century party in a brothel.

When they weren't drunk, the girls seem to have got on together like one big happy family. We read about them sharing their clothes together and having fights when one girl borrowed another's stockings without asking permission. Although the "house" girls never did any soliciting on the streets, they frequently attended masquerades, where they were often picked up by gentlemen who thought they were respectable women out for a good time. After a great deal of protesting, the girls would allow themselves to be seduced and then, amid tears and hysterics, demand a large sum for their ruined honor.

The end for these girls was usually the workhouse. Hogarth shows such a scene. The girls are pounding hemp with mallets. An overseer with a cane moves among them. One girl is hanging by her hands in the pillory, over which is written: "Better to work than to stand thus." The girl standing in the center of the picture is Mary Moffat, who was arrested for debt and dragged off to prison still wearing her brocaded evening gown covered with rich lace and silver thread. Hogarth sketched her from life.

A handful of these girls were able to rise above their environment, and a few even made brilliant marriages. Nancy Parsons, after being the mistress of the Duke of Dorset and the Duke of Grafton, married the wealthy Lord Maynard. Nancy used to boast that she had once received one hundred single guineas in a day from one hundred different gentlemen. Fanny Murray, the twelve-year-old girl who was seduced by Jack Spencer, married Mr. David Ross, a wealthy and respectable gentleman. Fanny always boasted that she had been one of the nuns of Medmenham. But these were the rare exceptions, although they were always held up to the "does" (as the novice prostitutes were called) as an example of what an ambitious girl could do.

In addition to the regular prostitutes there were the amateurs or "dollymops," as they were called. The dollymops were "respectable" girls who occasionally did a little soliciting on the side either to pick up pocket money or just for fun. It was to protect the dollymops that the Medmenham nuns were masked.

A dollymop was generally started on her career by being seduced by some man who afterwards deserted her. A popular dollymop ballad ran like this:

> "The first I met a cornet was
> In a regiment of dragoons,
> I gave him what he didn't like
> And stole his silver spoons."

The flower girls who sold flowers in the streets were often dollymops. So were milliners. Sometimes they worked out of "introducing houses." In these houses, meetings between girls and men were arranged by a go-between, although nothing improper was ever allowed to take place on the premises.

A few dollymops were prominent society ladies. The most famous of these was Miss Chudleigh. She was the mistress of the Earl of Bath and the Duke of Hamilton. She turned up at the Venetian ambassador's masquerade in the "character of Iphigenia." Miss Chudleigh's interpretation of this role was to wear nothing except a transparent, gossamer veil and a wreath of roses around her middle. She was later secretly married to the Earl of Bristol, but started living with the Duke of Kingston. Miss Chudleigh saw the chance of becoming a duchess, so she sneaked into the church where she had married the earl and tore the record of her marriage out of the register. She then married the Duke, who gave the Earl 50,000 pounds to keep quiet, but the Duke's family did some investigating and found out the truth. Miss Chudleigh was tried by the House of Lords for bigamy and narrowly escaped being branded with a hot iron. She was forced to leave the country and retired to the continent. There she lived with Frederick II of Prussia, the Prince of Radzivil, and several of the Russian and French nobility. In France, she bought a palace and settled down with her coachman. She died at the age of sixty-eight.

There were many stories told about her. Knowing her insatiable passion for sex, Sir Robert Keith remarked that he'd gladly marry the lady if a grenadier guardsman would join him in the nuptials. It was said that she'd given birth to illegitimate twins, and Miss Chudleigh asked Lord Chesterfield if he believed the scandal. The lord replied politely, "I make a point of never believing more than half of what I hear." When the Princess Augusta (the wife of Frederick, Prince of Wales, who was living with Lord Bute) reproached Miss Chudleigh for her private life, the young lady retorted in French, "Your royal highness knows that every woman must have her goal." The French for goal is *but*, pronounced "bute." Her reputation for doing everything double was so great that when a two-headed calf was born in Essex, Horace Walpole insisted that Miss Chudleigh must have given birth to the animal.

Compared with Miss Chudleigh, the poor girls who were forced into prostitution either by poverty or the machinations of the madams were quite respectable people.

The members spoke proudly of the "amoristic acrobatics" of some of the girls and described the various positions in great detail. From the descriptions, many of the prostitutes must have been expert contortionists and the monks pretty supple also. These various positions are illustrated in the *Kama Sutra* and in John Cleland's *Fanny Hill* (Cleland was a famous rake who lived at this time and may have attended the club's meetings). Some of them require three or four people working as a team to perform. Some of the positions also require apparatus such as the "musical balls," "night-caps," and "blessers."

One device which was provided for the ladies was the

Idolum Tentiginis or "lustful toy." This was a rooster hobby-horse with the beak in the form of a phallus, the bird's neck being turned around so his beak lay along his back. This Idolum Tentiginis was for the nuns to ride to get up their passions. For the male members, there was a small dispensary where aphrodisiacs could be compounded.

The monks were very proud of their potency. One member kept a score chalked up on the door of each monk's record for the evening. The nuns were well taken care of. A doctor and a midwife were kept in constant attendance on the premises not only to mix the aphrodisiacs and revive the members who passed out, but also to care for any nun who became pregnant. The doctor was Benjamin Bates, an esteemed local practitioner and a Scholar of Aylesbury. The children born to the nuns were called "The Sons and Daughters of St. Francis" and as they grew up they were given jobs around the abbey.

As might be expected, venereal diseases were common among the brotherhood. They used to address each other as Signor Gonorrhea and Monsieur La Croix de Venus (syphilis). Several died either of the diseases or from complications resulting from the infections.

At some time during the evening, a banquet was held in the Roman Room. Sir Thomas Stapleton calls these banquets "exquisite and Gargantuan." The table was spread with damask and glistened under the candelabra with the gleam of silver and fine cut glass. A special Hell-Fire punch was served in a silver bowl (the recipe for this brew has unfortunately not come down to us) and the bread was Holy Ghost Pye. The various dishes had colorful names: "Breasts of Venus" (two squabs served side by side with a single red cherry on top of each) and "Devil's Loins" (roast beef cut in the shape of buttocks). An incredible amount of liquor was consumed. The wine books for the club have recently turned up in Wycombe and show that each of the monks generally consumed three or four bottles of wine at a sitting. Two of the brothers drank four bottles of port, two of claret, and one bottle of Lisbon during a meal. Men were rated by the amount of wine they could drink, and a rake was referred to as a "three-bottle man" or a "four-bottle man," depending on his capacity.

The monks also drank special cocktails called "Strip Me Naked," "Lay Me Down Softly," and so on. The recipes have been lost, except that, judging from some of the names ("Gin and Sin," "Gin and Fanny"), gin was apparently the main ingredient.

So far, only the members' dissipations have been mentioned, but Sir Francis and many of the other members were intensely interested in other subjects besides liquor and women. Sir Francis founded the Dilettante Club which probably did more than any other group of the time to forward an interest in classical art. The club subsidized *The Antiqu-*

ities of Athens, by Stuart and Revett, the first important work on the ruins of ancient Greece, and also sent out the archeologist who discovered the ruins of Herculaneum and later of Pompeii. Dashwood and other wealthy members subsidized artists (including Sir Joshua Reynolds and George Knapton) and several young sculptors and poets who never reached such prominence. It was the rule of the group that whenever a member married, he had to pay the club a percentage of his wife's dowry. (No young gentleman of family ever considered marriage unless the lady brought him a substantial income.) This money was used to purchase rare antique vases, statuary, and old manuscripts, most of which were then presented to museums. Like all clubs of the time, the Dilettante was a pretty gay group. Walpole re-marked that the "nominal qualification for a member was having been in Italy, but the real one was being drunk." However, they accomplished a great deal for art and arche-ology. Many of the Hell-Fire group also belonged to the Dilettante.

Sir Francis organized another club which didn't resound much to his credit, but should be mentioned as an illustra-tion of the baronet's love of make-believe. This club was called the Divan. To join, you had to have traveled in Tur-key. The members dressed as Turks and held banquets to which ladies of easy virtue were invited. One of Dashwood's sisters was a member and was painted in her harem costume. Dashwood was grand master, and there was also an Imp who dressed in red, as the baronet loved a hint of the diabolical in everything.

Dashwood was no coward and always stood ready to back anyone who seemed to be getting a raw deal. In 1757, a British fleet under the command of Admiral Byng was ordered into action against a far superior French fleet. The action took place off Minorca and the English were defeated. Byng managed to escape with the remnants of his fleet, but the public, who liked to feel that the English were invincible on the sea, were furious and demanded a scapegoat. Byng was selected by the government as the sacrifice and sentenced to die. Mobs paraded through the streets singing, "Swing, swing, great Admiral Byng!" and the king, George II, let it be known that he would take any attempt to defend the Admiral as a personal affront. Both Parliament and the nobility followed the lead of the king and the mob in denouncing the friendless Admiral. Almost the only exception was Dashwood. Dashwood was a member of Parliament, although he seldom bothered to attend sessions (it was understood that townships always sent their local lordling to Parliament to represent them), and he defied the hisses and boos of his fellow members as well as the King's fury to defend Byng. He was denounced as a traitor, a friend of the

French, and a dangerous radical, but he kept on. In spite of Dashwood's efforts, Byng was shot. Voltaire sarcastically remarked that the unfortunate man had been executed "to encourage the other admirals."

2 Since the monks of the Hell-Fire Club included many of the most outstanding men of the day, the club became so popular that two different categories of membership were created: Superior and Inferior. The Superior members were the Twelve Apostles and, of course, Sir Francis. There were many more Inferior members, but they were apparently not allowed to take part in the chapel ceremonies except on special occasions, although they were given free run of the abbey and the nuns. There may have been as many as forty or fifty Inferior members, and everyone was permitted to bring an occasional guest, either male or female. When one of the Superior members died or went mad, the Apostles selected his successor from the Inferior

group. There was keen competition for this honor, and there was a great deal of jealousy and resentment when the choice was made known.

Except in a few cases we don't know with certainty who belonged to which group, as quite naturally the monks didn't boast of their affiliation with the notorious Hell-Fire Club, and the club's records were subsequently burned. In the following list, it has been taken for granted that the more active, prominent monks belonged to the Superior circle, although some may never have achieved that honor, and one or two may even have been virtual employees of Dashwood, hired to do the bookkeeping, arrange the banquets and bring in the girls.

Sir Francis Dashwood

Sir Francis, as well as being the founder, was the spirit and the head of the club. His pictures show that he was handsome as a young man, with dark, curly hair. He was well built, although inclined to be thick-set, and he was possessed of an eager, almost boyish enthusiasm which showed in his face. Horace Walpole says, "He was seldom sober but charmingly tolerant and frank." John Wilkes says, "He was the only one [of the Superior group] . . . to show real gifts of imagination and true mental abilities." Everyone, friend or enemy, agreed that he was honest and outspoken. They also agreed that he was an incurable exhibitionist. He was famous for his profanity in a time when no gentleman spoke without a collection of picturesque oaths. In the latter part of his life he became heavy with protruding eyes and dangling jowls. Unfortunately, most paintings of him were made during that period.

The Earl of Sandwich

Sandwich was Dashwood's right-hand man, the executive officer of the club. He was the most notorious rake of the day. He has been described as being "as mischievous as a monkey and as lecherous as a goat." Another writer remarked: "No man ever carried the art of seduction to so enormous a height." Sandwich specialized in seducing young girls, "the corruption of innocence being in itself my end," he boasted. His relations with women were "extensive and peculiar." He hired naked prostitutes to beat him across his bare bottom with whips to augment his flagging sexual drive. He was also called "the most universally disliked man in England." He was an inveterate gambler, often playing for twenty-four hours at a stretch and refusing to leave the table. On one such occasion he ordered a waiter to put a slice of beef between two pieces of bread and bring it to him so he could eat while still playing—thus inventing the sandwich that still bears his name. It is curious that the name of this sex fiend should have gone down in history connected to such an innocent article of diet.

Because of his title and through political influence, Sandwich was made First Lord of the Admiralty. The Sandwich Islands were discovered during his term of office and named after him. Curiously enough, in an age when most political appointees did absolutely nothing, especially if they were lords, Sandwich threw into the job the same savage energy he used in seducing schoolgirls, getting drunk, or celebrating the Black Mass. He arrived at the Admiralty office at six in the morning and worked until after dark, driving his subordinates as hard as he did himself. Then he'd spend the night at Mother Sulphur's bagnio or with the nuns at Medmenham, returning refreshed to his governmental duties. Unfortunately, he accomplished nothing except to get the service into such a mess that it took years to restore its efficiency. The *Encyclopaedia Britannica* describes his administration as "unique in the history of the British Navy for incapacity." He had a tremendous driving energy coupled with absolutely no intelligence, except for a certain craftiness in injuring others. He was sent as a roving ambassador to several countries, but a special committee had to be formed to follow him and correct the diplomatic crises he created.

Sandwich is described by most of his contemporaries as a man so ugly as to be almost deformed, but his early portraits (he was a member of the Divan Club and was painted by Knapton in Turkish costume) show him as having almost effeminate good looks. No doubt he changed as he grew older, due to the kind of life he led. He had at least one venereal infection that may have affected his brain. Even as a young man he was subject to nervous convulsions during which he lost control of his limbs.

Next to Dashwood, he was the most ardent antireligious member of the club. He once preached a sermon in a church to a congregation of cats. Like most of the rakes, he was desperately brave. He fought over twenty duels, usually with the husbands or fathers of his paramours, and was famous as a dead shot and an expert swordsman. One of his innumerable mistresses was Kitty Fisher, a famous courtesan of the time. Although Sandwich was keeping her ("acting as her protector" was the polite phrase of the period) Kitty was a gay girl and used to entertain other lovers without the Earl's knowledge. Once he arrived at her apartment unexpectedly while Kitty was entertaining Lord Mountford, who was himself a notorious rakehell. When Mountford heard that the Earl was downstairs, he begged Kitty to let him hide under her hoop-skirts. Kitty refused and Mountford jumped out of the window rather than face Sandwich.

In addition to being antireligious, Sandwich was violently antidemocratic. He despised the general public and opposed any public figure who tried to get a better break for the common man. Sandwich was a member of a small group known as the "King's Friends" who stood prepared to support the autocratic monarch on any issue whatsoever and override opposition to his wishes by the more liberal members of Parliament. Because of his friendship with the King and his control of the English Navy, Sandwich was one of the most important men of the time and exerted a profound influence on the destiny of the British Empire.

The Earl of Bute

Compared to the Earl of Bute, Sandwich was a rather lovable personality. Bute was another of the "King's Friends" and was made Prime Minister, thus becoming the most powerful man in the nation. Although as great a rake as Sandwich, he had none of Sandwich's dash and color. Thackeray says: "He was hated with a rage of which there have been few examples in English history." He never dared to appear in public without a bodyguard of prizefighters, and even so was nearly killed by mobs on several occasions. He opposed every reform measure, destroyed the Whigs (the liberal party), and ruined William Pitt, England's greatest statesman. He seduced the Princess Augusta (the wife of Frederick, Prince of Wales) and through her influence controlled the government even before he was made prime minister. Pitt spoke bitterly of "the secret influence more mighty than the throne itself which betrays and clogs every administration." Because of his control over the Princess, Bute had a large hand in bringing up her son George (who later became George III). He frequently told the boy: "Remember that when you are king you must be ruthless." George's attempts to follow this advice resulted in the American Revolution. Bute himself hated the American colonists. He supported the Stamp Act, opposed Edmund Burke's attempts to find a peaceful solution, and encouraged the King to use force against the American Colonies.

Bute's rise to power came about in a way typical of the time. Frederick, Prince of Wales, had gone to the races at Egham, but the races were delayed because of rain. The royal party decided to play cards while waiting for the rain to stop, and the Prince sent his equerry to find someone who'd make a fourth at whist. The equerry came back with Bute. During the game, Bute told the Prince about the Hell-Fire Club, and Frederick, who was a notable rake, was delighted. Bute introduced him to the club and Frederick became a member—or if he did not actually join, he was given the run of the abbey and frequently attended the meetings. This introduction established Bute with the prince, who subsequently made him Lord of the Bedchamber, a peculiarly appropriate appointment, as Bute then proceeded to knock up Frederick's wife, the Princess Augusta, a not too intelligent German girl. Frederick himself was about as futile an individual as ever breathed. His father (George II) referred to him as "The Booby," and his mother once remarked that she wished he was in hell. Prince Fritz cordially returned their feelings, openly hoping that his father would die so Frederick could inherit the throne, and writing spiteful fairy stories about a brutal king and his fat queen who wouldn't give their noble son enough money. The prince, however, died first, and it was his son who inherited the throne as George III. George III made Bute prime minister as a reward for the Earl's known attachment to his family.

Next to Dashwood and Sandwich, Bute was the most prominent member of the Hell-Fire Club. He never missed a meeting and went about getting drunk and fornicating in the simple, direct way he approached everything. He never seems to have shown much interest in either the Black Mass or the artistic side of the club. Probably he valued the organization for the satisfaction it provided his vices and the hold it gave him over the weak-minded Prince Fritz. Excepting George III, Bute was probably more responsible for the American Revolution than any other one man.

Paul Whitehead

Whitehead was the club secretary. It has been suggested that he was never a member, but was employed by Dashwood to keep the organization running. At all events, he was an important figure.

Whitehead was the son of a small tradesman and had neither title nor money. When he was in his early twenties, he backed a bill for a friend who promptly absconded, and

Whitehead was thrown into a debtor's prison for several years. He had always had a talent for writing verse, and now he began to write rhyming political lampoons (very popular in those days) for anyone who would pay him. As the wealthy Tories were better able to afford such propaganda than the Whigs, most of Whitehead's poems were directed against the Whigs, but he himself had democratic sympathies and often wrote poems attacking the King and the court on his own responsibility. He made enough to get out of prison and departed with the conviction that there was no justice in the world and that whatever happened, he was going to look after himself.

He supported himself by his political writings and made enough to do a little whoring and drinking on the side as well as to play elaborate practical jokes. The Freemason announced that they were going to stage a parade through London, and Whitehead dressed a collection of cripples, beggars, and prostitutes in Freemason robes and sent them ahead of the procession. Whitehead had an assistant in this elaborate masquerade—Henry Carey, who wrote "Sally in Our Alley" and the words to "God Save the King." The prank amused the Hell-Fire Club and they sent for Whitehead. Whitehead instantly attached himself to Dashwood. He was shrewd enough to realize that the baronet was so surrounded by flatterers that he'd welcome some opposition, and so Whitehead always made a point of standing up to

Sir Francis and only allowing himself to be persuaded that his patron was right after a long argument. He wrote a rhymed pamphlet in praise of immortality which he arranged to have attributed to Dashwood. The pamphlet made a big hit and Dashwood was delighted, but honest enough to deny that he was the author. However, Whitehead explained to the baronet that he'd only written down Sir Francis' witty sayings when he was drunk and the baronet accepted this explanation and acknowledged authorship of the best seller.

Whitehead was older than most of the other members (they called him "Old Paul") and in addition to ordering the meals, seeing that the nuns got in and out, and running the servants, he also acted as sexton during the Black Mass ceremonies, reminding the Abbot what to do next and handing him the proper texts. Whitehead composed most of the blasphemous hymns sung and was referred to as "the Atheist Chaplain" of the club. He kept the club's accounts, and Churchill, a member who was one of the most popular poets of his day, wrote:

"Whilst Womanhood in habit of a nun
At Mednam lies, by backward monks undone;
A nation's reckoning like an alehouse score,
Which Paul the Aged chalks behind the door."

Whitehead finally established himself financially by marrying a crippled, half-witted girl whose parents were willing to pay anyone 10,000 pounds to take her off their hands. Whitehead's associates naturally expected him to abandon the girl after he'd gotten her money, but he was always very good to her, making sure that she was comfortable and happy before going off for an evening with the nuns at the abbey. Sometimes he even took her along so she wouldn't be lonely. One evening during a sparkling interchange of wit between such brilliant talkers as Wilkes, Selwyn, Potter, and Churchill, the poor girl tried to join in the conversation by saying, "Oh gentlemen, I saw a cow today!" Whitehead, instead of trying to shut her up, instantly asked her to tell them more about the cow and, the rakes gravely listened while the pathetic little moron recounted her remarkable experience.

It's been said that Whitehead had more to do with keeping the club running than anyone, even Dashwood. If Dashwood was the soul of the organization, Whitehead was the brains and backbone. Whitehead was deeply attached to both Dashwood and the club. He willed Dashwood his heart after death, and his last act was to burn the club's records. Robert Lloyd, one of the brotherhood, called him "learned in lechery, a sedulous and patient seducer and a veritable troubadour of blasphemy."

Charles Churchill

Although few people read Churchill's poetry today, he was regarded by his contemporaries as one of England's greatest poets. Like Whitehead, he specialized in political satire, which was then highly regarded, but his allusions are too topical to be of interest now. The British Navy thought so highly of his work that flags were ordered lowered to halfmast the day he died.

Churchill (no relation to Sir Winston Churchill) was the son of a clergyman and was himself a priest in the Church of England. He was an enormously powerful man with abnormally thick arms and legs. An expert boxer, the club called him "The Bruiser" and Hogarth caricatured him as a grotesque bear. At the age of eighteen he had defied his family by marrying a street girl, by whom he had two children. His father insisted that he enter holy orders and as the boy was completely dependent on his family for support, he was forced to obey, although he hated the church and was an avowed atheist. Later he deserted his wife and children.

Like most of the brothers, Churchill was a curious mixture of the sentimental and the brutal. He fought for the debtors in Fleet Prison and started a home for destitute prostitutes, while at the same time, as Dashwood remarked, "peopling the house with young girls whom he had seduced." Although a clergyman, he was as big a rake as the others. Wilkes once wrote him, "Don't fail to make yourself known to Effie when in Tunbridge Wells. Mention my name and you will find her both pliant and pliable. She is gifted with a capacity for translating the language of love into a rich, libidinous, and ribald phraseology." Churchill was an ardent liberal and led the campaign against Bute, Sandwich, and the King in defense of the American colonists. He is described as being both remarkably good-natured and a bully. Once, while conducting a funeral service, he was jeered at by a man in the congregation who had seen him drunk with some girls the night before. Churchill peeled off his clergyman's coat, jumped out of the pulpit and beat the man into a pulp. One evening at the abbey, he got into a violent row with Whitehead as to who would have first go at one of the girls and, the men eventually became deadly enemies. Later he wrote:

"May I (can worse disgrace on manhood fall)
Be born a Whitehead and baptised a Paul?"

On the other hand, several men (notably John Wilkes and Robert Lloyd) were deeply attached to him, and he was spoken of as a true friend who would never let you down. As a democratic gesture, he always drank beer instead of wine, and insisted on consorting with the lowest type of prostitutes rather than fashionable ladies although he could have had his pick. Like many rakes, he suffered from a venereal disease. (He wrote Wilkes: "What I imagined to be St. Anthony's Fire has turned out to be St. Cytherea's.") He was cordially hated by the government because of his liberal tendencies and political satires.

Bubb-Dodington (Lord Melcombe)

Bubb-Dodington was an enormously rich, grossly fat, utterly dissipated individual who would do anything to be noticed by the aristocracy. He was the son of a poor chemist, but an uncle had died leaving him one of the largest fortunes in England. He was born simple George Bubb, but as he had some distant relations named Dodington, he tacked that name onto his own; it sounded more elegant. He obtained his title after a campaign seldom equalled for bribery and wire-pulling. Before the ceremony creating him Lord Melcombe, he spent hours in front of a looking glass in his new robes, practicing attitudes and debating with himself as to the most graceful way of carrying his coronet. Later he hired poets to write odes to the imaginary deeds of his fictional great ancestor.

Bubb dressed in silk suits with lilac waistcoats covered with heavy embroidery. Like most fat men, he had his suits made too tight in the hope of appearing thinner. Once, while bowing to Queen Charlotte on the occasion of her marriage to George III, he split his breeches up the seat. The queen made a noble effort to keep her face straight, but finally began to giggle, and the whole court burst out laughing. Bubb spent the rest of the afternoon backed into the porti-eres. He built a fabulous mansion for 140,000 pounds (about $700,000) not far from West Wycombe and also built a city house next to Prince Fritz's London establishment. The gardens of the two houses connected, so Fritz could sneak into Bubb's place anytime he wanted a gay evening. Bubb supplied the girls through an arrangement with Mother Sulphur and Mother Stanhope. Both the town and country houses were incredibly elaborate, with marble staircases, Gobelin tapestries, and handcarved woodwork. Bubb himself slept in a golden bed with a canopy of peacock feathers, surrounded by rows of Greek statues.

In spite of his wealth, Bubb was strangely stingy with women. He had a colored mistress, Mrs. Strawbridge, who demanded that Bubb give her a bond for 10,000 pounds to be paid her if he ever married. Bubb put up the bond, but then when he married he forced his wife to keep the marriage a secret so he wouldn't lose the bond. His wife had to live with him ostensibly as his mistress until Mrs. Strawbridge died.

Because of his intimacy with the Prince, Bubb had considerable political influence. The Prince used him as a butt for practical jokes, setting up elaborate booby traps for him and once having him wrapped in blankets and rolled down the steps of his own house. On another occasion, the Prince had him thrown into the Thames in the middle of winter. He used to borrow large sums from Bubb, then box his ears and burst out laughing at the fat man. Bubb didn't care as long as he could boast that he was a friend of the Prince of Wales.

Bubb was a great ladies' man, and his frantic efforts to match the other members' records with the nuns probably contributed to his death. In spite of his obesity he also tried to be a romantic seducer in the great tradition, but without much luck. In the boudoir of one fashionable lady, Bubb exclaimed dramatically, "Oh, if I only had you in the middle of a dark forest!" The lady tartly responded, "What would you do there that you can't do here—rob me?" He had the reputation for being a noted wit, although most of his sallies sound pretty feeble now, and even his friends admitted that his jests didn't sound so funny after being written down. Bubb had a lazy, drawling way of delivering a joke while slouched back in a chair with half-closed eyes that was very effective. Also, as everyone agreed, it was so astonishing to hear this mountain of blubber say anything intelligent that the surprise was more important than the joke itself.

At least one of Bubb's *bon mots* has stood the test of time. I heard it used by a TV comic a few weeks ago. Bubb had been talking to a nobleman and left him howling with laughter. Joining Sir Francis and Churchill, Bubb remarked,

"Lord X has really no sense of humor." Dashwood replied, "He seemed to be laughing hard enough at the joke you just told him." Bubb explained, "Oh, he wasn't laughing at *that* joke; he was laughing at one I told him three months ago. He just now saw the point of it."

Charles Churchill wrote this description of him:

> "Bubb is his name and bubbies doth he chase,
>   This swollen bullfrog with lascivious face."

George Selwyn

Selwyn is famous for the collection of letters he left, written to him by virtually every prominent man of the age. He was a noted humorist and has even been called "the first of the fashionable wits." When Lord North married a very fat bride, someone remarked that he didn't see how the marriage could be consummated in such hot weather. "Oh, the bride was kept on ice for three days," remarked Selwyn. A father, son, and grandson all had the same mistress, passing her on from one generation to another. "There's nothing new under the sun," some buck remarked. "Nor under the grandson," added Selwyn.

Selwyn was an ardent Satanist and an avid necrophilist (one morbidly fascinated by corpses). He was expelled from Oxford as a young man for walking into a tavern with a silver chalice which he'd stolen from a church and then cutting his arm and letting the blood run into the cup. He insisted that everyone in the room drink the blood, saying, "Drink this in remembrance of me." Selwyn's defense was that he had merely tried to ridicule the Catholic Mass.

There are many stories told of his love of death and suffering. He used to attend public executions disguised as an old woman so people wouldn't recognize him. He had a standing arrangement with undertakers to inspect the corpses brought in to them. While attending services at Westminster Abbey with some friends, the sexton greeted him with, "Oh, your servant, Mr. Selwyn. I expected to have seen you here the other day when the old Duke of Richmond's body was brought up." Selwyn went to a great deal of trouble to travel to Paris when Damien, a man who had attempted to assassinate Louis XV, was being tortured to death in the public square. Damien was to be nipped with red-hot pincers, broken on the wheel, and then torn limb from limb by horses, and Selwyn didn't want to miss the show. He arrived too late to get a front row seat, but the executioner recognized him and shouted, "Please let this gentleman through, my friends. He's a famous English amateur." When Lord Holland was on his death bed, he told the servants, "Should Mr. Selwyn call, show him up at once. If I'm alive, I'll be glad to see him, and if I'm dead he'll be glad to see me."

Selwyn was a regular visitor to the abbey, but apparently he came for the sake of the Black Mass rather than the nuns. There was even a rumor that he was a eunuch. He was a regular visitor to the more fashionable brothels, but he may have gone only to be whipped or to have the girls put on shows for him. However, he claimed to be the father of several bastards, including Maria Fagniani who later became the Marchioness of Hertford.

Thomas Potter

Potter was the son of the Archbishop of Canterbury and possibly the rottenest of the entire group. His father gave him 100,000 pounds (about $500,000) which he squandered on drink and women. He is particularly famous for having corrupted John Wilkes, the most brilliant political figure of the day, although Wilkes didn't seem to have need for much corrupting. He was spoken of as "Wilkes' evil genius." Potter boasted, "I poison all my friends' morals," and lived up to his boast. After running through the fortune left by his father, he married a wealthy wife and spent her money also. Afterwards, he beat her to death. For some reason, Pitt liked him and made the rake Vice-Treasurer for Ireland. Potter was also a great pal of Prince Fritz and acted as his secretary. Like Selwyn, he was fascinated by death and used to cohabit with his lady friends in open graves or inside tombs. He was also accused of having sexual relations with corpses.

He was an ardent Satanist, wrote psalms for the Black Mass ceremonies, and frequently served as chief priest at the altar. In addition, he was a member of Parliament, where he was outstanding for his brilliant speeches. He seduced the wife of the Bishop of Warburton and she had a son by him. The bishop never forgave him, which caused important political repercussions.

Other club members of less prominence than the above were: Robert Lloyd, a well-known minor poet, who died of a broken heart after Churchill drank himself to death. The Earl of Oxford, Horace Walpole's elder brother, who was a half-wit; Sir Henry Vansittart, who became governor of Bengal and sent the club the *Kama Sutra*; Robert Vansittart, brother of Sir Henry, and a professor at Oxford; Giuseppe Borgnis, the famous Italian painter; William Hogarth, the English artist; the Duke of Kingston; Laurence Sterne, the novelist; Edmund Duffield, the local clergyman, who later drowned himself; the Marquis of Granby; Sir Joseph Banks, president of the Royal Society; and The *Chevalier D'Eon*.

The Chevalier d'Eon, although not prominent in the club's activities, was certainly one of the weirdest person-alities in all history. No one knew whether he was a man or a woman. He dressed as both. He would attend the abbey meetings as one of the nuns and then reappear later dressed as a man and join in the fun. He was a famous swordsman and in duels killed several bucks who had dared to ask him his real sex. He was an undercover agent for Louis XV of France and conspired with several of the brotherhood (notably Bute and Wilkes) to overthrow the throne. At one time, bets as to his true sex ran so high (amounting to over 6 million dollars) that the Chevalier was in danger of being kidnapped by the heavy betters so his sex could be discovered by force. After once being drugged and several times attacked by armed gangs, he agreed to allow a jury of "respectable matrons" to examine him in the abbey. They returned a verdict of "uncertain."

3 The parties at the abbey must have been remarkable spectacles. As Thackeray says, "It was an era of wax lights, fine dress, fine jokes, fine plate, and fine equipages." The gorgeous Roman Room must have been ablaze with candles, lighting the salacious murals copied by outstanding artists from the 2,000-year-old Pompeian frescos. The members in their white robes lounged on the couches covered with fine green damask, while the nuns, naked except for their masks, poured their drinks into crystal goblets fashioned in obscene shapes.

Dashwood would be reclining on a couch at the head of the table, his handsome, eager face flushed with wine, with a nun on either side of him, describing how he had given Holy Communion to Lady Mary Wortley Montagu's pet monkey in the chapel.

Lady Mary was lying on another couch, although she was an elderly lady, listening with great amusement. She would leave the next day for Constantinople, where she was to write the series of letters on art, literature, gossip, and politics which have made her famous. Later, she was to introduce into Europe from Turkey the technique of inoculation against smallpox.

Bubb-Dodington was sprawled on another couch with a naked nun perched on his huge belly pouring vintage claret down his throat and giggling when he choked.

Thomas Potter was reeling around the room, bellowing out parodies of the Psalms.

William Hogarth sat quietly in a corner sketching his fellow members (the sketches would later appear in the "Rake's Progress" and the "Harlot's Progress").

Sandwich was screaming obscenities while making sure that the nervous fifteen-year-old nun supplied by Moll King's establishment was really a virgin.

The half-witted Earl of Oxford sat with a girl in his lap, mouthing gibberish while the wine ran out of his mouth. The Earl had been made a member of the club partly to add to the uncanniness of the general atmosphere and partly to annoy Horace Walpole, his younger brother, who despised the organization.

George Selwyn was repeating, in his usual languid manner, his immortal quip when asked by the prominent politician Charles Fox if he had attended the hanging of a notorious highwayman who was also named Fox. "Oh no, my lord," Selwyn had drawled, "I never go to rehearsals."

The Bruiser-clergyman-Poet Churchill, with a stein of beer in his hand and his bearlike arm around the toughest prostitute in the lot, was roaring:

"The grasp divine, the emphatic, thrilling squeeze!
The throbbing, panting breasts, the trembling knees!
The tickling motion, the enlivening flow!
The rapturous shiver and dissolving . . . oh!"

Meanwhile, servants hurried about with trays covered with exotic dishes molded into suggestive designs and gleaming with fine glass and silver. A messenger had just come from Italy with news of a priceless urn recently uncovered, and an express rider from Parliament was waiting outside with news of troublesome American Colonists, who, in spite of all orders, were fanning out into the Ohio Valley. One of the nuns was demonstrating a new position not found even in the *Kama Sutra*, and Sterne and Lloyd had got into a violent argument as to whether Capability Brown's handling of delphinium beds would have done for Petronius.

The initiation of a new member was an elaborate and dramatic ceremony. At midnight the candidate, clothed in a milk-white robe that flowed loosely around him, walked alone to the door of the chapel and knocked on the door. As it opened, he prostrated himself and then walked slowly to the altar rails, where he fell on his knees. The Apostles sat in carved chairs along the wall, and Sir Francis, in his priestly robes, attended by Paul Whitehead, conducted the ceremony. The narcotic herbs burning in the braziers filled the chapel with fumes that dimmed the light of the candles. The candidate was called upon to abjure his faith and then recited after Dashwood a perversion of the Apostles' Creed and the Articles of Faith. The candidate was sprinkled with a mixture of salt and sulphur and was baptized in a black font. He was then given some mystical name by which the brotherhood always referred to him during meetings. For example, John Wilkes was called "John of Aylesbury," as he had been elected to Parliament from that district.

After receiving the blood-red triangular Host, the candidate was finally admitted into full membership. Everyone then repaired either to the Roman Room or the Withdrawing Room, where the nuns and the supper were waiting.

As the descendants of these gentlemen are for the most part still very prominent in English society, historians have tried to excuse the antics of the Hell-Fire Club by saying that the members weren't much worse than most aristocrats of the period. It was indeed a colorful age. George II knelt by the bedside of his dying queen, sobbing so uncontrollably that she begged him to marry again. "Never! Nothing but mistresses!" wept the heartbroken monarch. Charles Fox lost 200,000 pounds ($1,000,000) gambling, and Lord Stavordale, twenty years old, lost 11,000 pounds (about $55,000) at a sitting and then recovered the whole sum by one hand. He shouted angrily, "Now if I'd been playing deep, I could have made some money."

Cheating at cards and dice was a standard practice. A young man sitting in on the play at Brookes', an elegant gambling house, noticed to his horror that a noble gentleman was cheating. "What shall I do?" he whispered to the man sitting next to him. "Back his play, you fool!" was the retort. Sheridan, the playwright, followed the custom of the time by being almost constantly drunk. One evening two friends led him to the front door of his house in Berkeley Square and left him. Looking back, they saw that he was still standing in the same position. "Why don't you go in?" they shouted. "I'm waiting until my door goes by again . . . then I'll jump through it," Sheridan replied with dignity. Many of these stories have become so famous that they've been told over and over again, generally accredited to some current humorist.

Human life meant little to the rakes. One buck bet a group of friends that a man could live under water. He kidnapped a passer-by, put him in a watertight barrel, and sank it in a lake. Unfortunately, he didn't know that a man uses up the oxygen in a barrel very quickly, and so when the barrel was brought up, the occupant was dead. "I've been swindled, let's try again!" shouted the buck, and so the experiment was repeated. This time the victim lived. A man fell down while passing Brooks', the fashionable coffee shop. The young bucks began to lay bets whether he was dead or not. When some passers-by tried to use restoratives, the bucks objected on the grounds that this affected the betting.

Yet it was a strong age. The year 1759, when the Hell-Fire Club was at its height, was called "The Year of Miracles." The English fleet had swept the seas. An obscure clerk named Clive conquered Bengal (annual revenues 2,000,000 pounds a year) with 350 men. England came to control one-third of the surface of the globe—America, Canada, the West Indies, Africa, and India. Of all this vast area, the richest was America. A steady flood of tobacco, fur, cotton, sugar, and timber poured from it. The "stately homes," as well as the sums paid to Mother Stanhope for her fifteen-year-old virgins, came from these revenues. Yet the American Colonists were difficult to handle. "We cannot control them as we can control the wretched peasants of India," shouted Pitt in the House of Commons, but too few Englishmen felt the same. Yet "Hell-Fire Francis" Dashwood was one of these far-sighted men. As sensitive as he was dissipated, he had a feeling for the rebellious colonists, perhaps because he, too, was a rebel.

Dashwood began to correspond with the American scientist, political pamphleteer, and philosopher Benjamin Franklin. Dashwood was always interested in new ideas, and the writings of this colonial struck him as being original and important. Also, Dashwood had just been made Postmaster General and Franklin was Postmaster of the colonies. At first, Franklin answered the letters in all seriousness, outlining his political views and the reforms he felt were necessary for governing the American Colonies, but he soon realized that Dashwood merely played with politics as he played with art and Satanism. Smart one that he was, Franklin instantly altered the tone of his letters. He knew something about the Hell-Fire Club through his various connections and was shrewd enough to realize the group's importance as a means of getting his ideas across to the English ruling class. But also he realized that the rakes couldn't be preached to. He accordingly adopted a different tone.

Franklin was said to have two illegitimate children and was credited with being the author of several papers on subjects such as "Advice to a Young Man on Selecting a Mistress" and "The Technique of Farting." His famous "Polly Baker letter" was an appeal to old maids to have as many illegitimate children as possible in order to build up the population in the colonies. He wrote: "Passion has hurried me frequently into intrigues with low women that fell in my way which was attended with some expense and great inconvenience because a continual risk to my health by a distemper which of all things I dread although by great luck I have escaped it." He was the author of several jolly poems, one of which runs:

> "Fair Venus calls, her voice obey,
> In beauty's arms spend night and day.
> The joys of love all joys excel
> And loving's certainly doing well."

Franklin was able to meet the Hell-Fire Club on their own ground. As far as any abhorrence of the Black Mass went, Ben announced that he did not believe in the immortality of the soul and he considered evil permissible, since God had created all things and so had presumably created evil also.

It is very doubtful that Franklin was as obdurate as he painted himself, but, as an expert politician, he could give people what they wanted to hear, and he knew that to a considerable extent the fate of the American Colonies lay in the hands of the men composing the Hell-Fire Club. Like most liberal men of the period he was suspicious of formal religion because the churches tended to support the ruling class. Even when he was an old man of eighty-four, he wrote to Ezra Stiles, the President of Yale, saying that he doubted the divinity of Christ, although he believed in His moral teachings.

Dashwood urged Franklin to come to England so they could discuss matters ranging from politics to sex. Ben was eager to go, but unfortunately for the course of history, he was unable to leave America.

In 1751, "Prince Fritz," the Prince of Wales who had taken part in so many of the club's orgies, died. The members paid a touching tribute to their deceased friend by throwing a giant brawl and reciting a poem to his memory which ended: "As it's only Fritz who's dead, there's no more to be said." Fritz, although a simple-minded, debauched youth, had refused to take the club too seriously. Once when Bute and Sandwich were lecturing him on how to keep the restless Colonists in order, the Prince had burst out laughing and exclaimed, "If I listened to you, I'd be the greatest stadholder (dictator) that England's ever known." But Fritz was dead, and his son George was a serious-minded youth with no vices except stupidity and pigheadedness. He listened eagerly to Bute and Sandwich and followed their advice. In 1760, when George II died, the son of Prince Fritz ascended the throne as George III. He was only twenty-two and hadn't been able to learn to read until he was ten.

The Hell-Fire Club played an important part in forming the young King's mind. Some of the members, like Dashwood, Churchill, and Lloyd, were highly intelligent men who knew that a policy of armed reprisals against the American Colonists would be useless. On occasion they stood up bravely for their beliefs, but they could always be distracted by a new cocktail, a new pornographic statue, a new variation on the Black Mass, or a pretty ankle. It was the men like Bute and Sandwich who deliberately used the power of the club to influence the young King. By now the club had at least one top-flight representative from every influential group in the country—art, literature, and politics. Though the great men of the day—Selwyn, Sterne, Vansittart, Hogarth, Walpole, and Fox—had their nobility, they also had their lusts. It was to these lusts that the club catered—sex, drink, gambling, and, more subtly, the desire to belong to a secret organization with elaborate, mystical trappings engaged in ceremonies too awful for even the young hell-rakes of Vauxhall and Ranelagh.

It was an age of revolt. The writings of the cynical Voltaire, who punctured the pretensions of the clergy and the established morality, delighted young men who prided themselves of being smart and knowing. The new doctrine of the "equality of man" propounded by Rosseau inspired many others. The industrial revolution had begun and the people were becoming a force to be reckoned with. Men were both frightened and fascinated by these new ideas. In the Hell-Fire Club, the conception of revolt was dramatized. The members could blaspheme God, see the Prince of Wales drunk with whores, watch England's leading artist sketch the scene, and listen to the most popular poet of the day compose dirty hymns. Yet when the fun was over, these same men would sit around a table and decide whether to start a war with Spain, complete the conquest of India, or forbid the American Colonists to go west of the Alleghenies. The combination of debauchery and genius was irresistible to the smart young men of the 18th Century. And clever men could use the power of the club to advance themselves politically.

When George III became king, almost his first act was to make Bute his prime minister and Sandwich the First Lord of the Admiralty. He then made Dashwood the Chancellor of the Exchequer. Even Dashwood was amused by the appointment, which, unlike the other two men, he had not sought. "I'll be the worst chancellor England ever had," he told his friends at a riotous meeting in the Abbey, but Churchill solemnly disagreed with him. "You have had considerable experience with figures, my Lord," the poet remarked slyly. "You have often helped Whitehead chalk up how often each of us have had a go at the nuns."

4 The hell-fire club was now virtually running the country. The unhappy young King couldn't find his bottom with both hands while the mad geniuses who composed the club could do anything from writing *double entendre* verses in Greek to ruining an opposing statesman by a clever satirical sketch. The club might have continued indefinitely on its merry way had not a deterring element managed to creep in. This element, was composed of one man—John Wilkes.

John Wilkes was a great exponent of democracy and the rights of the common man, so his biographers have united in describing him as having a great heart under a rough exterior. The exterior was certainly rough. He was a skinny man (his opponents in duels protested that they couldn't see him when he turned sideways)—and he had a twisted mouth over a protruding jaw. He was also equipped with a villainous squint, although one of his innumerable mistresses defended his looks on the grounds that he didn't "squint more than a gentleman should." Wilkes himself had no illusions about his appearance. He once remarked, "Well, thank God I'm not likely to fall in love with my own image like Narcissus." His looks did not prevent him from being one of the most outstanding seducers of the age, and even Sandwich regarded him with grudging admiration. Wilkes once boasted, "Give me half an hour's start to make up for my face, and I'll seduce a woman ahead the handsomest man in Europe." To settle bets in the club, he often gave demonstrations of his powers. Once he even beat out the famous Casanova by knocking up a reigning beauty whom the great lover had been trying to make for six months. Casanova devotes an entire chapter of his memoirs to the event.

Wilkes was born in 1727. His father was an ex-distiller who drank himself to death, and he had two sisters, both mentally deranged. When Wilkes was twenty-one, he married a dull, respectable lady in her early thirties who was ugly as pig tracks but possessed a handsome fortune. "It was a sacrifice to Plutus [the god of money] rather than to Venus," Wilkes frankly observed in a letter to a friend. His wife didn't seem to mind her husband's going to the local bagnios, but when he started bringing his girls home and throwing parties that lasted all night, she became peeved. Finally she left him. At that time, a woman's money automatically became the property of her husband as soon as she married, but Mrs. Wilkes' lawyers managed to talk Wilkes into giving his unfortunate lady an income of 200 pounds a year from her estate. In return, she had to sign a paper giving Wilkes complete freedom and promising never to bother him again. Later, Wilkes tried to stop even the 200 pounds, which would leave his wife completely destitute, but the courts wouldn't let him. Wilkes was always furious over this gross injustice.

Wilkes had one child by his wife, a little girl named Polly. He was devoted to the child. When she caught smallpox, the highly infectious and then generally fatal disease, his wife and all the servants fled from the house, leaving the dying child alone. Word was sent to Wilkes, who was whooping it up at Charlotte Hayes' brothel, and he at once rushed to the bedside of his daughter. He nursed her day and night until she recovered. After the breakup with his wife, Wilkes kept Polly and was always very good to her, even though it occasionally meant having to short-change some of his current mistresses. Wilkes was also good to his bastards, which was unusual at that period. He had two illegitimate children and always saw that they were clothed and fed.

Thomas Potter is generally credited with having introduced Wilkes to the Hell-Fire Club. While Wilkes was in the midst of his row with his wife, Potter wrote him: "I'm escaping from the solemn lullabies of my mother-in-law and the yells of a young female Yahoo that has thrust herself into the world yesterday. [Potter's wife had just presented him with a baby girl and he was a proud father.] If you prefer young women and whores to old women and wives, come and indulge the heavenly inspired passion of lust."

Wilkes answered his friend's invitation without delay and Potter took him to the Medmenham abbey. There he met the nuns, or, as Potter called them, "the sweet little satin-bottoms." Wilkes became an enthusiastic disciple of the group.

Many of the members regarded Wilkes with considerable distrust. He was obviously a smart young fellow on the make, and he had no title and no money except the remnants of his wife's fortune. They also resented the fact that he was smarter than they were. Dashwood, however, took an instant liking to him. Wilkes was brilliant, amusing, an atheist, an extreme left-wing politician, and utterly immoral—all qualities that Sir Francis admired. Dashwood even made Wilkes a colonel in the Bucks Militia, a swagger regiment that Sir Francis had created, an organization that wore magnificent uniforms and never did any fighting.

Wilkes threw himself heart and soul into the club and

soon became very popular. He was a great wit, had an enviable fund of dirty jokes, and even composed some of the club's obscene hymns. He contributed a silver chalice with an obscene design that cost 20 pounds. (The bill for it turned up among the club's records some two hundred years later. Wilkes had never paid for it.) Eye-witness descriptions of this remarkable man give a good picture of him:

Edward Gibbon, the author of *The Decline and Fall of the Roman Empire*, wrote: "Colonel Wilkes dined at our mess. I scarcely ever met with a better companion. He has inexhaustible spirits, infinite wit and humor, and a great deal of knowledge, although profligate in principle as in practice, his life has been stained with every vice and his conversation full of blasphemy and indecency. These morals he glories in, for shame is a weakness he has long since surmounted. He told us himself that he had entered politics to make his fortune. This proved to be a very debauched day. We drank a good deal both after dinner and supper and when at last he retired, Sir Thomas Worsely and some others broke into his room and made him drink a bottle of claret in bed."

Charles Johnson later wrote severely: "He [Wilkes] had such a flow of spirits that it was impossible ever to be a moment dull in his company. His wit gave charm to every subject he spoke upon. The vanity which had first made him ambitious of entering society, only because it was composed of persons superior to his own rank in life, afterwards made him despise them. His humor was often debased into buffoonery and his wit was so prostituted to the lust for applause that he would sacrifice his best friend for a scurvy jest in which he was assisted by an expertness in carrying his jests into execution."

Johnson was right. Wilkes was continually in hot water because of his humor. He made a mortal enemy of Samuel Johnson by writing a comic review of the great man's immortal dictionary. Johnson had included some remarks on grammar in which he said: "The letter 'h' seldom, perhaps never, begins any but the first syllable." In his review Wilkes wrote "The author of this observation must be a man of quick appre-hension and of a most compre-hensive genius," and so on for several paragraphs. Johnson never forgave him.

One of Wilkes' jokes nearly got him killed. At George III's coronation, a certain Lord Talbot, in his role as lord steward, had to ride a horse into the royal presence, say his piece, and then back the horse out of the room so the King would never be affronted by the sight of the horse's rear end. Talbot had a trainer spend weeks working on the horse so the animal would be sure to back up properly. On the day of the coronation he prepared to gallop up to the throne in fine style. Unfortunately, the horse had been so well trained that he refused to do anything except back in, so the astonished King saw nothing but the animal's rump throughout the entire ceremony. Wilkes considered the incident hilariously funny and wrote a skit on it. This was a mistake. Talbot was not only a prominent amateur boxer but also a famous duelist. He was popularly called "The Butcher." After the skit appeared in the papers, Wilkes spent the night at the Medmenham Abbey and returned to his London house exhausted from the nuns and so drunk he could scarcely make it through the front door. In the living room, he found Talbot waiting for him with a brace of pistols and two friends. Wilkes gives an account of what happened in a letter to a friend:

"I found his lordship in an agony of passion. He said that I had injured him and that he was not used to be injured or insulted. Did I or did I not write the skit? He would know, he insisted on a direct answer; here were his pistols. I replied that I desired to know by what right his lordship catechised me. As for the pistols, he would soon use them.

"His lordship then asked me if I would fight him that evening. I said that I preferred the next morning. [Wilkes was in no condition to stand, let alone fight duels.] His lordship replied that he insisted on finishing the affair immediately. I told him that I should very soon be ready but would first settle some important business relative to the education of my only daughter, whom I tenderly loved.

"I rang the bell for pen, ink, and paper. After they had

been brought and I had made my will, I proposed that the door of the room might be locked and not opened till our business was decided. His lordship became quite outrageous, declared that this was mere butchery and that I was a wretch who sought his life. [Talbot had figured on fighting the duel in the open at a distance of several yards while Wilkes, who was too drunk to aim, wanted them to fire at point blank range.] He said to me, 'You are a murderer, you want to kill me, but I am sure I shall kill you. I know I shall, by God! If you do kill me, you will be hanged. I know you will.'

"I knew that his lordship fought me with the King's pardon in his pocket and I fought him with a halter about my neck. [Wilkes meant that if Talbot killed him, the King would never let his lord steward be hanged, but if Talbot was killed, Wilkes would certainly go to the gallows.] But I would fight him for all that. He then told me that I was an unbeliever (referring to the Hell-Fire Club) and wished to be killed. I could not help smiling at this and observed that we did not meet to settle articles of faith but points of honour.

"I again desired that we might decide the affair in the room but he was quite inexorable. I agreed to fight in the garden. Our seconds then charged the pistols, which were large horse pistols. It was agreed that we should fire at the word of command.

"We then left the inn and walked to the garden at some distance from the house. It was near seven and the moon shone bright. We stood about eight yards distant and agreed not to turn around before we fired but to continue facing each other. The word was given. Both our fires were in very exact time but neither took effect. I walked up immediately to his lordship and told him that I now avowed the paper. His lordship paid me the highest encomiums on my courage and we retired to drink a bottle of claret together."

This story shows Wilkes at his best—absolutely calm although opposed by a famous duelist, able to goad Lord Talbot into an impossible situation, and finally able to save his own life by a concession that did not reflect on his courage.

Wilkes' reaction to the Hell-Fire Club is interesting. Nearly everyone who came into contact with the monks of Medmenham responded in one of two ways. Either he was inexpressibly shocked and rushed away muttering about "unthinkable obscenities" or else he became convinced that Sir Francis and the rest of the brotherhood were the most whimsical, brilliant, fascinating group in the world. Wilkes' reaction was simply: "I was full of astonishment that any man should take so much pains and be at so great expense only to show a public contempt of all virtue." He was amused by the "Garden of Sin" and even copied down the Macaroni Latin mottoes which he considered clever (that's how we know what they were, since no other record has been left). He enjoyed the wine, free meals, and the nuns. As an atheist and ardent foe of religion, he had no objections to the Black Mass, but regarded it as an unnecessarily elaborate practical joke. He was astonished to find that the other brothers, especially Dashwood, took the ceremony very seriously and went about the whole complicated ritual with great solemnity and as if they really hoped to summon up the devil by their hocus-pocus.

Wilkes was determined to enter politics. At that time, politics was almost the only field offering any chance of advancement to a young man with neither family connections nor money. Wilkes' first attempt to get himself elected to office had ended in failure. He had run in the Beswick elections of 1754, even bribing a sea captain who was bringing a cargo of opposition voters from London to land his passengers on the coast of Norway. But Wilkes had been beaten. Now, however, with the support of the Hell-Fire Club, Wilkes decided to try again.

Through the influence of Thomas Potter, Wilkes was elected to Parliament as representative of the Borough of Aylesbury. Wilkes had no connection with the borough that he was supposed to be representing, but ward-heelers could be bribed to deliver a borough to anyone paying them enough money. Getting his borough cost Wilkes 7,000 pounds—almost the remainder of his wife's fortune. Dashwood thought that he'd been wildly overcharged, but Wilkes was satisfied.

Wilkes was a highly successful politician. He was possibly the first man to recognize the growing power of the people—"the mob," as they were contemptuously called by the nobility. Together with two of his Hell-Fire Club pals— Charles Churchill (the rough-and-ready poet-clergyman), and Robert Lloyd (the young poet who was Churchill's shadow)—Wilkes started a newspaper called *The North Briton*. The paper catered to the public taste by attacking unpopular measures (such as the tax on hard cider), praising the "common man," and occasionally taking sly cracks at the nobility, although Wilkes was always careful not to go too far.

In the Hell-Fire Club, Wilkes was selected to write going-away speeches about members traveling on the continent or to the colonies. Here's one he composed on Lord Sandwich who was departing on a trip to Spain:

"I hope that in Spain you will carry every breast-work, take the *demilune* (a mound covered with cut bushes to impede infantry), and plant your victorious standard in the citadel of every fair donna. Do not repeat the error of your lordship's great ancestor who unfortunately was lost, for in his last wonderful achievement he went to the bottom." (Lord Sandwich's grandfather had been accused of sodomy.)

Everything would probably have continued to go smoothly if it hadn't been for what Johnson called "Wilkes' willingness to sacrifice his best friend for a scurvy jest."

For some time, Wilkes had been growing continually

more irritated by the elaborate and boring ceremony of the Black Mass. He came to the abbey to get drunk and enjoy the girls. He didn't enjoy sitting in a robe watching the other brothers capering about in front of the altar, screaming blasphemies and daring God to prove that He existed by sending the devil to carry off their souls. It affected him much the same way Dashwood was affected by the penitents in the Sistine Chapel pretending to flog themselves with toy scourges. Wilkes despised hypocrisy and he decided that what the Black Mass celebrations needed was a little excitement. He made up his mind to provide it.

One of the members was Sir Henry Vansittart, who had gone to India as Governor of Bengal. Sir Henry sent the club a pet baboon as a mascot. It so happened the day that the baboon arrived Wilkes was alone at the abbey except for a couple of girls. He got rid of the girls and determined to give the brothers a Black Mass that they'd never forget.

He hid the baboon in his own home and got a tailor to make up a complete devil's suit for the animal—horns, tail, and the works. Then, with the help of an old manservant who worked at the abbey, he smuggled the baboon into the chapel dressed in its devil's suit. The baboon was hidden in a large chest that held the ornaments and utensils used for the ceremonies. The chest fastened with a spring lock and Wilkes tied a string to the lock and led it under the carpet to his own seat. He cut a hole in the carpet, so he could get hold of the string at any time.

Wilkes then left the abbey, returning that evening by barge on the Thames with the other brothers. Donning their white robes, the monks marched to the abbey and took their places in the chapel. The chapel, which had been carefully designed to look spooky, was lighted only by a few candles burning behind panes of reddish glass and was full of the drifting smoke wreaths from the braziers of burning herbs. The brothers had indulged in considerable preliminary drinking on the way down from London and were feeling pretty high. Wilkes waited until several of the monks were capering before the altar, ironically imploring their master, the devil, to come among them and receive their adoration in person. Dashwood elevated the bogus Host and the members fell on their knees in mock reverence. Wilkes knelt with the others and secretly pulled the string, releasing the baboon.

The frenzied animal came flying out the chest and took one bound onto the altar. The brotherhood, who had been concentrating on Dashwood, had no idea where this apparition had come from. For a paralyzed instant they stared at the gibbering monster and then a horrified yell, "The devil! The devil!" went up. The half-drunken men staggered to their feet and tried to run, but before they could escape the baboon had made another flying leap and landed on Lord Sandwich.

Mad with fright, Sandwich tried to tear the animal loose,

but the baboon clung to him, chattering with rage. Sandwich ran about the room screaming, "Spare me, gracious devil! You know I never committed a thousandth part of the vices of which I boasted. Take somebody else, they're all worse than I am. I never knew that you'd really come or I'd never have invoked thee!"

Someone opened a window and the baboon jumped through it. Sandwich fell on the floor half fainting. Most of the other monks were still running around the room screaming with fear. Dashwood had collapsed by the altar, still clutching the fake Host. The nuns, hearing the commotion, ran in to see what was happening. On hearing that the devil had actually appeared, the nuns promptly became hysterical and the entire abbey was a madhouse of screaming women, weeping men promising to mend their ways, and distraught servants rushing about with smelling salts and brandy pick-ups.

When the group finally calmed down, two or three members who had been in the back of the chapel and kept their wits about them announced that the apparition had been nothing but an ape dressed in a devil's suit. As the other monks gradually recovered from their terror, they began to think things over and decided that the creature's behavior had been more simian than diabolic.

"Where did the creature come from?" roared Dashwood, who had gotten a bad fright and was now furious. For some reason, he didn't consider this trick nearly as funny as his own exploit in the Sistine Chapel when the worshippers had mistaken him for the devil.

"Probably through the open window," suggested Wilkes who was having a hard time keeping a straight face.

"No, I opened that window to let him out," protested one of the monks.

It didn't take long to find the open chest and the string. The old caretaker was then dragged in and forced to confess. His excuse was that the monks loved to play practical jokes on him and the other servants, so he thought that no doubt they'd consider this jest equally amusing. The brothers couldn't see the logic behind this argument at all. Luckily for the old servant, they saved most of their rage for Wilkes. "What can you expect from the son of a distiller and a political pamphleteer?" yelled Sandwich. "He should never have been allowed in the club. Expel him!"

To give Dashwood credit, he held out against expelling Wilkes. Once he had recovered from his fright, the Baronet began to laugh at himself and admit that the joke had been a good one. He even had the baboon recaptured, and for many years it was "regarded as an object of veneration" by the brothers. But the other members wouldn't be appeased. Either Wilkes went, or Sandwich, Bute, Bubb-Dodington, and several other important brothers would resign. The argument went on for weeks, but finally Wilkes was expelled for "insulting the dignity of the club." The other members then took a solemn oath to have no more horseplay during the sacred Black Mass ceremonies.

Wilkes continued on friendly terms with Dashwood and a few of the other brothers, but most of the monks never forgave him. Sandwich was especially vindictive. When he'd recovered from his faint and found that the devil was a baboon, Sandwich had spent the rest of the evening trying to regain his reputation as a hardened hell-rake by wild speeches full of the filthiest blasphemies and by grotesque exhibitions with the nuns. Sandwich's outburst when the baboon leaped on his back had revealed him as a fundamentally deeply religious (or, if you prefer, superstitious) man. In spite of his cynical manner, he had a profound belief in the forces of evil and an all-abiding terror of eternal punishment for his sins. Dashwood had exhibited precisely the same traits when the two cats had got into his room in Rome. When Dashwood discovered that he had made a fool of himself, he underwent the violent reaction that resulted in the creation of the Hell-Fire Club. Sandwich now underwent a similar reaction but directed towards Wilkes.

Wilkes didn't give a fly's belch what Sandwich thought. He'd grown tired of the monks' antics and was glad to be free of the organization. Churchill and Lloyd continued to work with him on *The North Briton*, and Dashwood, the only other member whom he respected, remained his friend. Also, now that he had been kicked out of the club, Wilkes felt free to use for political purposes the wealth of scandalous material that he had picked up at the club's meetings to attack Bute, Sandwich, and even the King.

Wilkes was a Whig, a member of the liberal party, George III hated the Whigs and had created in Parliament a small but powerful group (many of them Hell-Fire members) called the "King's Friends." This group was sworn to support the King's policies under any and all conditions. Their first job was to destroy the Whigs: Under Bute's direction, this group had attacked individual Whigs, although they took care never to oppose the Whigs as a party and thus show their hand. The King's Friends' greatest triumph had been to drive the brilliant William Pitt from office and have Bute appointed prime minister in his place. This move had a profound influence on America, as Pitt had always been a staunch friend of the colonists, while Bute and the rest of the King's Friends were equally determined to rule by what the dead Prince Fritz had called "the stadholder policy."

Wilkes had always been sympathetic to the colonists. He had been corresponding with James Otis, John Hancock, and Josiah Quincy. These men assured him that unless the American Colonies were given representation in Parliament, they would fight. Wilkes had attempted to plead the Americans' case before Parliament, but had always been shouted down by the King's Friends. Now, through the medium of his paper *The North Briton*, Wilkes decided to strike back, using some of the secrets he had picked up during the drunken orgies at the Hell-Fire Club.

The Seven Years' War (fought in America as the French and Indian War) had just been concluded by the Peace of Paris (1763). Due to the stupidity of Bute and the King, the peace terms had been miserably mismanaged, and in spite of many great victories and an enormous expenditure of men and money, Britain received only a small part of what her army and navy had won. The defeat of the French in Canada left the American Colonists free to expand westward, but the short-sighted King, in order to preserve the fur trade with the Indians, issued a royal proclamation forbidding migration west of the Alleghenies. There was great popular resentment against the peace terms, and Wilkes decided to take advantage of the unrest.

In the famous 45th issue of *The North Briton*, Wilkes published a murderous attack on the government. After telling the scandalous story of Bute's affair with the King's mother, he then turned to the Peace of Paris. "It must indeed be the 'Peace of God,' for surely it passeth all human understanding," he cracked. He went on to describe the King as an idiot controlled by rakes like Bute, Lord Temple, and Sandwich. About the only one of his old associates whom he spared was Dashwood. He ended with an appeal to the public not to let the country rest in the hands of the King's Friends. If these men remained in power, he warned, all liberal institutions would be gradually destroyed.

Not even Wilkes could have foreseen the effect of "Number 45," as that issue of the publication came to be called. Furious mobs burned jackboots in the streets (Bute's name was pronounced "boot"), together with petticoats (a reflection on the memory of the King's mother). The raging King demanded Wilkes' arrest on the charges of libel and treason. The King's Friends heartily agreed, but as the offending article was unsigned and there was no direct proof that Wilkes had written it, the government decided to arrest not only Wilkes but also Churchill, Lloyd, and even the printers, under what was called a "general warrant." The general warrant was an archaic but still technically legal device by which the King could order the arrest of anyone thought to be associated with a criminal act, without having to mention names. Technically, a general warrant gave the King almost unlimited power to arrest political opponents. For many years the power had not been used, but now the King's Friends decided to revive it.

Constables were sent to Wilkes' home to arrest him. While the officers were going through his private papers looking for incriminating evidence, Churchill walked in. With great presence of mind, Wilkes said, "Ah, good afternoon, Mr. Thompson. And how is Mrs. Thompson? No doubt you are going to join her soon in the country." Churchill hadn't heard about the general warrant, but he took in the situation at a glance. "I'm on my way there now," he said, and walked out. After burning all papers showing his connection with *The North Briton*, he left for Medmenham by post chaise.

Wilkes was thrown into the Tower of London. His arrest provoked the worst riots London had ever seen. George Selwyn, who was accused of having had a part in the attack on Wilkes, was beaten up and rolled in the gutter. Nobles were dragged from their sedan chairs, turned upside down, and had "45" chalked on the soles of their shoes. The King himself was pelted with rotten fruit when he appeared. The mobs tore through London, smashing the windows of every house that didn't have "45" prominently displayed. For the first time the cry of "Wilkes and Liberty" was raised—a cry which was to haunt the King and his friends for many years to come.

Because of the popular clamor, Wilkes had to be liberated from the Tower. He was astonished and delighted by the whole affair. Wilkes had merely meant to pay off some old scores in the 45th *North Briton* but now he found himself the most popular man in England. He sent appeals to what he called "the inferior classes," begging them to support his gallant attack against the injustices of the general warrant and the tyranny of the King's Friends. The mob responded nobly. They caught Lord Bute while he was entering Parliament and nearly killed him. They also attacked Lord Talbot, who promptly peeled off his coat and knocked two rioters down. When the King went riding in his royal coach, the mob smashed the windows. When he got back to the palace, the King removed a stone from the inside of his cuff, where it had stuck, and presented it to Lord Onslow as a souvenir of the occasion.

The King's Friends decided that they couldn't make the charge stick against Wilkes for the publication of "45." There was too much popular feeling against the general warrant, and also the yarn about Bute and the King's mother was something that nobody wanted to see fought out in court. Wilkes' attack on the Peace of Paris was, after all, a legitimate political position. But the King was half mad with rage (he eventually did go completely mad, and many considered that Wilkes had helped to shove him over the borderline), so something had to be done. The King's Friends decided to take a leaf out of Wilkes' own book and use his membership in the Hell-Fire Club against him.

Many of the King's Friends were also either members of the club or had attended its meetings, but they had an angle. While still a member of the club, Wilkes had composed a long poem for the edification of his fellow monks, called *An Essay on Woman*. The poem was a parody on Pope's *Essay on Man* and was extremely filthy, like all Hell-Fire poems. The members had been so delighted with this composition that they'd asked to have it printed, and Wilkes had had thirteen copies made—one for each of the twelve apostles and one for Dashwood. In addition, he had included some Black Mass hymns which Wilkes had composed, using as a frontispiece a large phallic symbol with a wide head to resemble a cross, so the volume would appear to be a hymnal. Under the "cross" was printed "Saviour of the World." The little book was dedicated to Lord Sandwich and the poem began, "Awake, my Sandwich!" in imitation of Pope's "Awake, my St. John!"

The first four lines (about the only part of the poem that can be reprinted) go like this:

"Awake, my Sandwich, leave all meaner joys
To Charles [Churchill] and Bob [Robert Lloyd] and those
    poetic boys.
Let us, since life can little more supply,
Then just to kiss, to procreate, and die."

This poem is still considered so terrible that special permission has to be got from the Board of Governors to see a copy at the British Museum, and then it has to be read in a special room with a guard standing by. Actually, the poem is not really so terrible, but by modern standards it can't very well be reprinted. Briefly, the story is how Satan seduced Eve in the Garden of Eden, as Adam was too innocent to know what to do. The poem ends, "And ever since then, if a woman can't get it anywhere else, she'll go to hell for a good loving" . . . or words to that effect. It is interesting to note that within the last year a European motion picture company put out an animated cartoon with this same theme and the picture was banned by the United States government.

The King's Friends decided to use this poem, together with the pornographic hymns that accompanied it, to ruin Wilkes. As the book had been printed, the King's Friends could claim that Wilkes had intended to distribute it as a means of destroying religion and undermining national morality. Although the depraved habits of the rakes were pretty well known, Wilkes' *Essay on Woman* went beyond anything the ordinary churchgoing Englishman could tolerate. The existence of the Hell-Fire Club was a closely guarded secret and could not be betrayed, but the King's Friends felt that simply reading the poem in Parliament, without giving the circumstances under which it had been written, would be enough to fix Wilkes.

Through a curious lack of humor, it was decided to have Sandwich read the poem in Parliament, because it had been addressed to him. Sandwich, of course, was the most notorious rake in England, and he had to hire bodyguards to hold off the crowd of furious husbands and indignant fathers who followed him around. He was also famous for his blasphemy, and Horace Walpole once remarked, "Sandwich can never get rid of the smell of brimstone." His sneering, arrogant attitude had made him "the most hated man in London," and his mishandling of the British Navy, resulting in the death of hundreds of seamen, was notorious. However, the King's Friends picked Sandwich to denounce the poem in Parliament, and Sandwich, who had never forgiven Wilkes for the baboon episode, agreed, as long as he could omit the opening line which plainly showed that the poem had been intended mainly for him.

The reading of *The Essay on Woman* marked a turning point in English history. It occurred on November 15, 1763. Ever since the general warrant, Wilkes had had the English people and the liberal element in Parliament solidly behind him. Pitt, although defeated by the King's Friends, was now planning to stage a comeback with Wilkes' support. If Pitt returned to power, the demands of the American colonists would be met and all danger of revolution avoided. Wilkes was also set on breaking the power of the little group of noble rakes who controlled the government and establishing the liberal party in power. This meant that a minister like Grenville (who was responsible for the Navigation Acts and later the "Intolerable Acts" that touched off the American Revolution) would have to go, the power of the half-mad king would be curbed and Sandwich's steady destruction of the Navy would be stopped. Wilkes, although by no means the greatest of statesmen himself, had the popular touch, and the truly great statesmen were prepared to rally around him. Even more important was the psychological situation. Wilkes had raised the banner of revolt against the entrenched classes who were running the nation. If he succeeded, a new era of liberalism would appear in Great Britain. If he failed, people and statesmen alike would be convinced that it was hopeless to fight the King's Friends.

When Sandwich stood up in Parliament with the slender volume of poems in his hand, the King was in disgrace and the King's Friends were in discredit. It seemed nothing could stop the triumph of "Wilkes and liberty." There was only one power that could turn back the clock—the Hell-Fire Club, who could prove that Wilkes was a blasphemer and a degenerate, thus making it impossible for any decent man to support him. So this small group of brilliant, depraved men held the fate of England and America in their hands.

Sandwich began by announcing that there had come into his hands a poem which "violated the most sacred ties of religion and decency." This provoked a hearty laugh but the first Lord of the Admiralty began to read *The Essay on Woman*. Before he had got very far, the horrified Speaker tried to stop the reading, but the delighted members shouted "Go on! Go on!" Sandwich finished the poem and then announced gravely, "I was never so shocked in my life!" This remark from England's most notorious hell-rake convulsed the house. Dashwood, who was in the house as the representative for his district, denounced Sandwich's hypocrisy. "I never expected to hear the devil preaching!" he shouted. The elegant Lord Chesterfield, whose letters to his illegitimate son are still considered the most perfect examples of worldly wisdom, rose and turned back the fine lace at his cuffs, took a delicate pinch of snuff from his famous tortoise-shell box which was inlayed with a scene showing Leda being raped by the swan, and announced: "Thank God, gentlemen, that we have a Wilkes to defend our liberties and a Sandwich to protect our morals."

Now occurred one of the most famous exchanges of all time. Sandwich turned to Wilkes and shouted, "Sir, you will either die on the gallows or of the pox!" Wilkes rose and bowing politely retorted, "That, my Lord, depends on whether I embrace your principles or your mistress." A score of members were now on their feet, all shouting together. One man demanded of Wilkes, "Sir, do you consider this vile poem amusing?" Wilkes replied, "If I laughed, I laughed alone," meaning that he had never intended it for general circulation.

The King's Friends now produced two unexpected aces they had been holding back as a last reserve. One was a disreputable clergyman named Kidgell who was private chaplain to the Earl of March, one of the most famous rakes of the period. Kidgell's congregation had thrown him out because of homosexual relations with choirboys, and he himself had written a pornographic book called *The Card* which had nearly gotten him bounced from the church. He acted as the Earl's pimp. Kidgell announced that as a clergyman, he "was extremely offended at what he had heard and hoped that proper means would be taken for the punishment of so avowed an enemy to society."

Now Bishop Warburton rose. It may be remembered that Potter, who introduced Wilkes to the Hell-Fire Club, had once seduced the Bishop's wife. Potter and Wilkes had been great friends and, it was rumored, had collaborated on the poem. To point up the joke, Wilkes had included in the volume a number of pompous footnotes, supposedly written by the bishop, who in the role of Adam denounced the devil (Potter) for seducing Eve. The King's Friends made sure that the Bishop saw these footnotes. The Bishop didn't think them funny at all. So he joined the attack on Wilkes. First the Bishop, in all seriousness, put his hand on his heart and announced to the House that he had definitely *not* written the notes. They were a low forgery. He then went on, "No one, in my opinion, but the devil concocted the contents of such a production," and then, after a dramatic pause, added, "I beg the devil's pardon, for I do not think even him capable of so infamous a production."

The opinion of two clergymen, one a bishop, could not

be ignored. The House agreed to delay action against Wilkes on the double charges of blasphemy and indecency, but meanwhile the King's Friends saw to it that copies of *The Essay on Woman* were secretly offered for sale all over London. Printers, knowing a good thing when they saw it, hurriedly rushed into print with bogus "essays" hastily written by hired hacks. These fake poems were, if possible, even more salacious than the original. However, they were less amusing.

So many of these fake essays were circulated that it's impossible now to tell what was the original version. One essay was dedicated to Fanny Murray (she was the twelve-year-old flower girl who was seduced by Jack Spencer and had grown up to be one of London's most famous prostitutes) and begins, "Awake, my Fanny!" Fanny was being kept by Lord Sandwich when *The Essay on Woman* was first written and it was suggested that Wilkes originally wrote the essay to amuse Fanny, who was two-timing Lord Sandwich with Wilkes. This has been offered as an explanation of why Sandwich was so determined to ruin Wilkes. Several very learned articles have been written on this question and other problems concerning the famous essay which, if you have time to spend, you can read for yourself, checking them against the known versions of the poem which are kept in locked vaults in various parts of the world.

Since Wilkes knew as much about Sandwich, Bute, and

the homosexual clergyman Kidgell, as they knew about him, it may be asked why he didn't retaliate by revealing their private lives. The answer is that Wilkes could no more ruin these men's reputation than he could sink the Swiss Navy. They were all notorious rakes. They were, however, either lords or under the patronage of a lord (as in Kidgell's case). Wilkes was on his own and had become the exponent of the honest, true-blue Englishman fighting against degeneracy in high places. For him to turn out to be as bad as the others robbed him of popular support. Wilkes' friends tried desperately to explain that they were supporting Wilkes' principles while denouncing his private life, but it was difficult to support a Satanist and writer of obscene literature as the symbol of British virtue. Even Pitt, who had always been Wilkes' supporter and friend, rose in the House to call the author of the essay "a blasphemer who did not deserve to be ranked among the human species." Thus Wilkes lost the support of the honest members of Parliament who were his own sympathizers.

While Parliament was debating what to do about Wilkes, Lord Sandwich was expelled from the fashionable Beefsteak Club. During dinner the noble lord had recited a poem of his own composition which, experts agreed, was far worse than anything in *The Essay on Woman*. While Wilkes' supporters were busy shouting about the immorality of the man who had dared to attack their hero, word came from Churchill, Wilkes' partner in *The North Briton*, who had been hiding out in the country. It seemed Churchill had kidnapped and raped the young daughter of a stonecutter and needed Wilkes' help to escape prosecution.

So far it was a stand-off—Sandwich's lapse against that of "The Bruiser" clergyman, Churchill. The verdict still might go for Wilkes in Parliament, so the King's Friends determined on an extreme measure.

An obscure member of the House named Samuel Martin suddenly felt called upon to rise and denounce Wilkes as a "coward and malignant scoundrel." These were fighting words and could mean only one thing—a duel. Wilkes, whatever his other failings might have been, was no coward. He instantly sent a message to Martin demanding a retraction. Martin wrote back saying, "I repeat that you are a malignant scoundrel and now I desire to give you an opportunity of showing me whether the epithet of cowardly was rightly applied. I desire that you meet me in Hyde Park immediately with a brace of pistols each to determine our differences."

Wilkes got his pistols and went to the park at once. Martin was waiting for him with his seconds. The party had to walk some distance through the park before finding a secluded spot. Then they prepared for the duel.

The duelists stood back to back with their pistols in their hands while one of the seconds called, "One . . . two . . . three

. . . and so on up to seven. As each number was called, the men took one step in opposite directions. When they were fourteen paces apart, the second called, "Cock your pistols, gentlemen!" Two clicks sounded. The second cried, "Ready! Turn! Fire!"

Martin missed. Wilkes' pistol failed to go off. According to the code, the seconds asked if honor was now satisfied. Wilkes said that was up to Mr. Martin. Martin, rather surprisingly under the circumstances, as he had no personal grudge against Wilkes, replied, "No, gentlemen, this duel is à l'outrance (to the death)."

Wilkes instantly replied that he was ready for another exchange of shots. Another brace of pistols was produced and the men fired together. Wilkes missed but he was hit in the groin by Martin's bullet. He fell to the ground, apparently mortally wounded.

Martin and the seconds ran over to him. Wilkes was lying in a rapidly growing pool of blood. "Fetch a doctor!" shouted one of the seconds. "It is useless! I am killed," Wilkes replied feebly. Martin was bending over him and Wilkes told his adversary: "You have behaved like a man of honor. I hold no grudge. Get out of the country or you will have to stand trial for murder." (Dueling, although common, was technically illegal.)

Wilkes managed to reach inside his coat and pull out Martin's note challenging him to the duel. "Burn this so there will be no evidence against you," he gasped. Martin snatched the note and ran.

Wilkes was taken to his home and a doctor was called in. It was found that Martin's bullet had been deflected by two buttons on his coat and so had not inflicted a fatal injury, although Wilkes had lost a great deal of blood and was in a serious condition. Martin fled to France. The King's Friends announced that Wilkes, in addition to being a devil-worshipper and a traitor to the king, was also a bully who had tried to murder the innocent and respectable Samuel Martin, but for once had met with his just deserts.

Wilkes later discovered that Martin had been hired by the King's Friends to kill him. Martin had spent the last few months constantly practicing with a pistol. Under ordinary circumstances, Wilkes would have the right to name the weapons and might have chosen swords. Martin therefore had hit on the device of sending Wilkes a note in a tone of high moral indignation daring him to come to Hyde Park immediately "with a brace of pistols each to determine our differences," knowing that Wilkes was hot-headed enough to accept the challenge without realizing that he was being tricked into using his opponent's pet weapon.

Wilkes was undisturbed by the tumult. He even wrote to a friend: "A sweet girl whose resistance I have for some time been trying to overcome has now written me that she feels safe in entrusting her honor to a man who has such a high regard for his own." Wilkes was never to keep his date with the sweet girl. The King's Friends managed to force a bill through Parliament declaring Wilkes an outlaw for high treason against the King, blasphemy, and circulating indecent literature. To get the bill passed, the King's Friends were forced to pack the house with elderly lords who were rushed to London from Bath, from hospitals and from the seclusion of their country estates. Chesterfield remarked that the House "looked like a restroom." Even so, Wilkes was declared an outlaw by a majority of only 44 votes.

Wilkes had guessed what the verdict would be. With his faithful companion Churchill, he had already fled to France. He was declared an outlaw in his absence and was forbidden ever to return to England.

5 The repercussions of the 45th *North Briton* were still great. Bute was ruined. Dashwood lost his position as Chancellor of the Exchequer, not because he had turned out to be "the worst chancellor in history" as he had prophesied, but because the government was now very leery of Hell-Fire Club members. However, the grateful King George made him Lord le Despencer—the premier baron of Great Britain—"to decorate his fall," as Wilkes unpleasantly put it. Dashwood was too important a man for even the King to offend. Sandwich was also forced to resign from the Admiralty, although he was reappointed a few years later.

The Hell-Fire Club, however, continued on its merry way and its members were preparing for a spectacular

comeback when a blow hit them from a completely unexpected direction.

A book called *Chrysal, or The Adventures of a Guinea*
appeared and instantly became a sensational best seller. The
book was a sort of 18th Century *Confidential* with the
guinea telling the story itself. The guinea would be lying on
the dressing table of the beautiful Lady C——— when Lord
L——— climbed in the window only to find the Honorable
Sir W——— R——— in bed with the lady. While the
maids were mopping up the blood from the ensuing duel,
Lady C——— would tell the second footman to take the
guinea and get her a shot of brandy. Naturally, the footman
would arrive at the winesellers just in time for the guinea
to overhear a conversation between Baron M——— and
Captain E——— of the C——— st———m Guards giv-
ing the real inside dope on what happened when the elderly
Duke of B——— found his young wife in a box-stall with
the groom. On one of its journeys, the guinea belonged to
a member of the Hell-Fire Club and so got the chance to
witness a Satanic ceremony and an orgy with the nuns.

The author of *Chrysal* was a man by the name of Charles
Johnson. He was never a member of the club and no one
knows where he got his information. It probably was from
Charles Churchill, who was leaving the country with Wilkes
and, needing money, sold the information. The description
of the abbey contains some obvious inaccuracies which

were almost certainly put in to throw curiosity seekers off the track. If so, these tricks failed in their purpose. Until the publication of *Chrysal*, the existence of the club had been known only to a select group in the upper crust of society, but once Mr. Johnson's novel hit the stands, everyone was determined to have a look at the abbey. The real location of the abbey was quickly discovered and tourists began arriving by carriage loads and by barge on the Thames. The abbey servants couldn't handle the crowds who overran the Garden of Lust and even tried to break into the abbey itself.

Maintaining a secret society under these conditions was difficult. When the robed monks left their barges in the evening for the solemn parade into the abbey accompanied by the ghostly tolling of the bell, the banks of the river were lined by sightseers who had come down from London for the day with picnic baskets. Not even the most ardent Satanist can get in the right mood for the awful ritual of the Black Mass when onlookers are shouting: "Pull that one's hood off, 'arry. Jim an' me has got a bet on whether 'e's the Marquis o' Granby or th' Earl o' March." For a while, it looked as though the club was through. But due to the genius of its founder, it now rose to its greatest heights.

Sir Francis—or Lord le Despencer, to give him his new title—decided to move the entire club to his estate at Wycombe. But where would the members meet? True, Sir Francis' mansion was big enough to house fifty Hell-Fire Clubs, but it didn't have the right atmosphere. There was no use building another abbey. An abbey was old stuff now, and, besides, the public would hear about it and come trooping down from London. No, something new was needed, something really spooky, unusual, and proof against trespassers.

Sir Francis hired workmen to dig out an elaborate system of caves laid out in the form of a sexual design (if Sir Francis had a fault, it was a one-track mind) in the side of a hill overlooking his estate. By the time this project was finished, the cave system ran a quarter of a mile into the hillside and enough material was excavated to pave a road from West Wycombe to High Wycombe, a distance of some eight miles. So the caves did *some* good. The project was so vast and required so many workmen that Sir Francis' defenders have even claimed that he had the caves dug in a benevolent effect to prevent unemployment in the district.

To the north of the little village of West Wycombe stands the hill in which the caves were dug. The hill is about 200 feet high and is part of a long, low range running east and west. The village is nestled against the base of this range, with a little stream called the Wye running past it. The village dates back to the 12th Century and is very picturesque with its houses with thatched roofs, its winding streets and colorful old inns. On the other side of the Wye from the hill is West Wycombe Park, covering some 200 acres. The house stands in the middle of the park on a little rise, overlooking a lake laid out in the shape of a swan and facing towards the hill. The house is hidden from the village by a magnificent woods of oak, beech, and ash trees.

The house was designed by the greatest architects of the period—Robert Adam, Nicholas Revett (a member of Dashwood's Dilettanti Club), John Donowell, and Atterbury. There are two stories. The main façade of the mansion is 240 feet long—a colonnade of 40 Doric pillars, surmounted on the second floor by a similar colonnade of Corinthian columns. The west portico was a copy of the Temple of Bacchus in Greece, the first attempt to incorporate Greek architecture into an English manor house. (The result has been widely imitated.) The east portico contained the grand salon, the largest room in the house, roughly about 100 feet long by 40 feet wide. The ceiling is completely covered by an enormous painting of "The Banquet of the Gods," based on the Raphael designs for the Villa Farnesina in Italy. Dashwood brought the famous Italian artist Borgnis over from Rome to do the job. The colors are as fresh now as when it was painted. In addition, there are four oval medallions showing scenes from the legend of Cupid and Psyche and four great oblong panels of the "Triumph of Galatea."

Italian plasterers were also imported to do the stucco friezes that encircle the room, and the chimneypiece and door frames are of imported colored marble, covered with carving by Scheemaker and Cheere. A dado of carved mahogany runs around the room. On the walls are paintings after Raphael, Caracci, and Guido Reni. There are two suites of Louis XVI furniture, covered with Beauvais tapestry. Huge French windows open onto the garden.

I won't describe all the other rooms in detail, but I'd like to give a general impression of the place. The west portico (or Temple of Bacchus) is only slightly smaller than the east and the ceiling is covered by a painting of "Diana in her Chariot." There is also the Tapestry Room (especially built for George III when he came down for a week-end), The Dining Room (also with a great ceiling painting plus a chimneypiece of white Carrara and Sienna marble inlayed was jasper), The Brown Drawing-room (overlooking the lake and used as a portrait gallery), the Blue Drawing-room (walls hung with giant mirrors in gilt frames, gold brocade curtains, and a ceiling panel depicting "The Triumph of Ariadne" attended by fauns, satyrs, and bacchantes), the Library (bookcases by Chippendale), the Grand Staircase (of red mahogany inlaid with yellow Yew), and the Great Hall (walls covered with paintings by Hogarth, Zoffany, and Romney). On the second floor were the bedrooms. The furniture is so massive that the floor could hardly support it. While Dashwood was showing Wilkes through the house, he remarked, "I think this furniture should be on the ground floor." Wilkes retorted, "Don't worry, it soon will be."

Many of Sir Francis' friends considered the house a little on the modest side. Mrs. Lybbe Powys, a fashionable lady of the period, remarked, "The house is nothing remarkable tho' very habitably good." I can only suppose that Mrs. Powys must have lived in a house that was a combination of Buckingham Palace and the Parthenon. However, although fashionable society might regard the house as too simple for a gentleman of means, everyone was impressed by the grounds. Even today the garden is regarded as one of the most perfectly balanced landscaping compositions of all times. Lawns, as green as emeralds and as smooth as a billiard table, led down to the swan lake. There is a little island in the center on which stands a tiny but exquisite Greek Temple. Woods surround the lake on the three other sides. Flowerbeds, studded with Greek statues and fenced by carefully clipped boxwood hedges, spread out to the south of the house, interspersed with little pools and fountains often connected by rustic bridges. Paths of soft moss led to small Greek temples set about the grounds; the Temple of Flora, the Temple of Daphne, the Temple of the Four Winds (a copy of the Horologion of Andronicus in Athens), and the Temple of Music. There was even an ornamental canal with gondolas floating on it. There were also Water Gardens, Wildflower Gardens, and Wood Gardens hidden away among the trees where lovers could stroll in complete seclusion or swim by moonlight in the marble pools.

The lake was so large that Dashwood kept a full-rigged ship on it as a sort of toy for his visitors. To celebrate the opening of the Temple of Bacchus, he staged a grand out-of-doors pageant in which actors and actresses dressed as priests, priestesses, Pan, fauns, satyrs, and bacchanals danced through the grounds and into the temple. The performers were dressed in animal skins, wreathed with vine leaves, and crowned with ivy to give an authentic touch.

Of course, Dashwood being Dashwood, he added a few little touches not commonly found in formal gardens. It has already been mentioned that the garden was laid out in the form of a nude woman. Another novelty was a temple which, although it was probably the most famous of Sir Francis' architectural triumphs, is hard to visualize from contemporary descriptions. Wilkes gives the following account:

"The entrance to it is the same entrance by which we all come into the world and the door is what some idle wits have called the Door of Life. Lord Bute particularly admired this building and advised the owner to lay out 500 pounds to erect a Paphian column to stand by the entrance."

Dashwood followed his friend's advice and the column was erected. It was, as Lord Bute had suggested, a huge phallic symbol, brightly painted. When Mother Stanhope sent the club some nervous young virgin who had been forced to sell herself, a favorite gag was to tell the girl that she would first have to pass an initiation ceremony and then take her out into the garden by moonlight and show her the pillar. Anything done to the girl after that came as an anticlimax.

There were a few other works of art of a distinctive nature scattered about the grounds, but unfortunately there is no record of what they were. The usual comment is simply that they were too obscene to describe.

Remaining today on the other side of the Wye River (in England, anything bigger than a trickle is called "a river"), are the caves running deep into the heart of the West Wycombe Hills. The entrance to the caves is shrouded by sepulchral group of tall yews, always associated with death and burial. The entrance itself is composed of flint triangles and pyramids set into the chalk rock of the hill. An iron gate with a heavy lock guarantees privacy. Beyond this gate a vaulted passageway leads into the heart of the hills. To one side of the passage, a room called the "Robing Room" is carved out of the chalk. Here the monks used to put on their habits before going deeper into the earth. It is said that in the caves instead of the white gowns they used at the abbey, they wore blood-red robes. Holding their lighted candles, they marched in single file deeper and deeper into the caves.

On the walls were carved devils' faces, and sculptured heads of demons were set into the chalk. The monks then came to a system of tangled passageways called the "cata-combs." No one knows why Sir Francis had these catacombs dug unless he was trying to imitate the famous catacombs in Rome. They give the place an eerie atmosphere, and with-out a guide it is a problem to find the way through them.

Beyond the catacombs comes another long, narrow pas-sage which leads into the Banqueting Hall. This room, the largest man-made chamber ever carved in chalk, is 50 feet high and 40 feet in diameter. From a hook in the center of the domed ceiling hung the Rosicrucian lamp which Dash-wood first got in the George and Vulture and had hung in the abbey. Opening off this room are "cells," small rooms just large enough to hold a bed. Curtains hung in front of these cells so the occupants could have privacy. There's a small recess in each cell where clothes can be hung.

In the center of this room, directly under the lamp, stood a huge refectory table. It was overhung by a canopy in case bits of chalk from the ceiling became dislodged by the shouts of the roisterers. When the monks met in the Ban-queting Hall, this table gleamed with fine silver and glass. Footmen in powdered wigs and brilliant livery waited on the guests, serving food prepared in the great kitchen of Wycombe House. Just beyond the Banqueting Hall is the Buttery where great hogsheads of wine were stored.

No ordinary visitors were ever allowed beyond the Ban-queting Hall. On the far side of the room still another passageway leads to the Triangle. This triangle, which is in the lower part of the cave system, is not simply a triangular room. Instead, the passageway divides, one passage leading to the right and the other to the left. After running a few yards, the passages turn sharply and rejoin, thus forming the triangle—a sexually significant pattern.

Beyond the Triangle, a river runs across the passageway. At the time of the monks, this river was so wide it could only be crossed by a boat which was kept moored to the bank for this purpose. The brothers called it "The River Styx." Beside the river is a well sunk deep into the chalk and called "The Cursing Well." It is filled with what the monks called "unholy water" and here the initiate was baptized. After crossing the river by boat, the brothers then went down a short passage into the "Inner Temple"—a circular room in the very deepest part of the hill. Here the Black Mass was celebrated and a solemn sacrifice made to the devil of the virginity of the young girls lured into the cave system. Wilkes, who was later allowed to partake of these ceremonies after his return from France, wrote: "A village maiden said good-by to her innocence when she visited the Inner Temple."

Hidden in this cave system, the Hell-Fire Club was able to resume its interrupted routine. They didn't have to worry about sightseers. No one could get past the iron gate and besides it would have taken a pretty hardy sightseer to wan-

der through that labyrinth with the devil's head grinning at
him from the walls and to swim the river to find out what
was going on in the Inner Temple.

It was mentioned the caves were laid out in a sexual
design. Dr. G. B. Gardner, a well-known British expert on
the occult who had the famous Witches' Museum at Castle-
town on the Isle of Man, describes the symbolism. "The
swollen Banquet Hall represents the womb, where new life
originates. After being born in the womb, the worshippers
pass through the pubic triangle and into the flowing river.
Then born and purified, they go on to the joys of resurrec-
tion that await them in the Temple."

According to a popular legend there's a secret passageway somewhere in the caves. There was one passage that
led from the caves to a church which Sir Francis built on
top of the hill. The clergyman, Timothy Shaw, used this
passage to take part in the ceremonies and conduct the
Black Mass. This was after the club's first minister, Edmund
Duffield, had drowned himself from remorse. This passage
is now clogged by fallen pieces of chalk but the steps can
still be seen. Miners who were hired by the baronet, Sir John
Dashwood, to make some repairs in the caves in 1954 reported being able to feel a draught of fresh air coming down
the passage.

But was there another passageway? Cut in the wall between the Robing Room and the Catacombs are the letters

XXIIF . . . in other words, the Roman numeral 22 followed by the letter F. What does it mean? There's no explanation for the F unless it stood for Francis but there's a curious old nursery rhyme song by the Wycombe village children:

"Take twenty steps and rest awhile;
Then take a pick and find the stile
Where once I did my love beguile.
'Twas twenty-two in Dashwood's time,
Perhaps to hide this cell divine
Where lay my love in peace sublime."

While Dashwood was busy digging holes in hillsides, Wilkes returned to London. He was still under sentence of outlawry but that didn't bother him. During his absence, the King's Friends had made such a failure of governing the country and handling the rebellious American Colonists that the public was disgusted with them and the King. Wilkes was reasonably sure that the government would not dare to have him arrested for *Number 45* and people would have forgotten about his *Essay on Woman.*

Wilkes returned alone. Charles Churchill, the drunken clergyman poet and cofounder of *The North Briton,* had died after a prolonged drinking bout in France, muttering, "What a fool I've been!" Churchill's poems had been so popular that when news of his death was announced the British fleet lowered their flags to half mast. Wilkes intensely mourned his friend's death and tried to raise enough money to get Churchill's collected poems published. He failed. Wilkes himself was in desperate financial straits. He had hardly enough to maintain the beautiful Italian courtesan, Corrandini, whom he was keeping. Corrandini was one of the reigning beauties of the day and came high. Wilkes' beloved daughter, Polly, had followed him into exile, and his sympathizers have often pointed out that Wilkes always saw to it that Polly was clothed and fed even though the expense of supporting the girl might cost him the affections of Corrandini. Wilkes' supporters in Great Britain and America sent him money and he was able to pick up some small change by writing pamphlets denouncing the English government.

Wilkes went from court to court in Europe, trying to ingratiate himself with the ruling house, generally by offering to spill the dirt about the corrupt habits of the British nobility gleaned from his Hell-Fire Club information. As the antics of the monks of Medmenham were fairly well known among the European nobility, most of whom had attended club meetings while touring England, Wilkes didn't get anywhere and the continental aristocracy was suspicious of any man who had been able to denounce a king and survive the experience. Madam Pompadour, the mistress of Louis XV of France, asked him wonderingly, "Monsieur Wilkes, just how far can an Englishman go in insulting the King and still live?" Wilkes bowed low and replied, "That, madam, is what I'm attempting to find out."

Madam Pompadour had a right to be puzzled. In France, any man who even criticized the King would have found himself inside the Bastille in short order. There would have been no talk about the legality of a "general warrant." The King would simply have issued a "lettre de cachet" for his arrest and imprisonment. There were forms signed by the King sentencing any one to the Bastille for life. They were issued with the name of the condemned left blank, and the King used to pass them out among his favorites so they could have anyone who they disliked sent to prison for an indefinite period. Although the British government of the time was corrupt and high-handed, it must be remembered that compared with other governments of the period it was remarkably indulgent—not only in its treatment of Wilkes but also in its handling of the American Colonists. Men like Patrick Henry, John Adams, and Benjamin Franklin would have gotten short shrift if they had been under Louis XV, Frederick of Prussia, or Maria Theresa of Austria.

Not that the King's Friends wouldn't gladly have gotten Wilkes out of the way if they'd had the power. There were several attempts to have him legally assassinated by led captains—professional duelists analogous to the gunhands of the American West a hundred years later. Once while

Wilkes was going with Lord Palmerston to watch a religious procession at the Cathedral of Notre Dame, he was stopped by a man who called himself "Captain Forbes." This man claimed that Wilkes had written some articles in *The North Briton* criticizing the Scotch, and, as Captain Forbes was Scotch, he demanded satisfaction. Wilkes replied that he had never written such an article. Forbes retorted that anyhow he must apologize.

"I will not apologize to you or any other man," Wilkes retorted.

"Then you must fight me today," returned Forbes.

Here Palmerston interposed and asked Forbes to what regiment he belonged. Forbes said he was with a French regiment. Wilkes explained that he was already bound to fight a duel with Lord Edgemont, an English lord who had challenged him as a result of *No. 45*. "As soon as I have settled with him, I'll fight you," Wilkes told him.

"You're a coward," roared Forbes.

That was more than Wilkes could stand. "Come to my hotel at noon with your seconds and we'll go to the dueling ground," he said.

At noon, Wilkes was waiting with his two seconds when Forbes turned up alone. Forbes explained that his seconds would meet them on the ground. This was contrary to all dueling etiquette as the seconds had to arrange, ahead of time, the place, the weapons, and the manner in which the duel was to be fought, so Wilkes became suspicious. At this point, Palmerston hurried in to say that he had checked through the French army lists and could find no "Captain Forbes." Forbes said that he had been cashiered from his regiment and his name had been stricken from the lists. Palmerston now wanted to call off the whole affair but Wilkes told Forbes that if he could get someone to act as his second, Wilkes would still fight him.

A few days later, Forbes sent word that a Mr. Murray would act as his second. Wilkes' friends urged him not to go ahead with the duel, as Forbes was obviously a professional hired to kill him. They also reminded him of his duty to let Lord Edgemont have first go at him. While Wilkes was hesitating, word came from England that Edgemont had died. Wilkes said furiously, "What a scoundrel trick he has played on me! I wished to send him to the devil but now he's gone without my passport."

Wilkes at once wrote to Mr. Murray asking him to arrange the duel with Forbes. He also wrote to his well-wishers in London: "Do not think I hold myself obliged to fight every dirty Scot, but I choose to show what I can do with such a fellow as Forbes." He never got an answer from Mr. Murray. Probably there was no such person. Wilkes spent the next three weeks trying to find Forbes, even advertising in the newspapers for him, but Forbes had disappeared.

There was therefore general rejoicing (except among the

DANIEL P. MANNIX

King's Friends) when John Wilkes, after making suitable provisions for his daughter, turned up in London in the spring of 1769. Dashwood called him down to Wycombe at once, and a big party was held in the caves to celebrate his return. All the London madams responded nobly to the challenge. Mrs. Hayes, an educated lady who kept one of the higher class brothels, wrote coyly to George Selwyn: "Mrs. Hayes presents her most respectful compliments and takes the liberty to acquaint that tomorrow evening at 7 p.m. 12 beautiful nymphs, unsullied and untainted, will perform the celebrated Rites of Venus as practiced under the instruction and tuition of Queen Obera, in which character Mrs. Hayes will herself appear upon this occasion."

The party was a great success. Several members fell into the Cursing Well and nearly drowned and the nuns were voted a sensation. Wilkes demonstrated some new tricks he had picked up while abroad. It was later reported, "There was no corruption that he had learned anywhere but he was able to duplicate it."

Unfortunately, we don't know the details of these parties, which might give us an interesting sidelight on the nature of the club members. The orgies were apparently recorded in the club's minutes but Paul Whitehead burned the book just before he died. Another copy turned up 30 years later but was also hastily burned. We do know the emphasis that the club put on securing virgins for the parties. This was typical of the times. Deflowering virgins was a mania with 18th Century rakes. It seems to have been a pathological craving with them. Another outstanding passion was for flagellation. In fact, the French referred to flagellation as the "vice Anglais." Highly technical treatises were published on this business, complete with suggestions of how to make the paddles, whips, and birches. Many of the rakes had to be flogged before they could show any interest in women. These men had used up their energies by ceaseless dissipation and could only respond to some drastic treatment. Fanny Hill speaks of a thirty-year-old nobleman who had already become almost impotent. This was typical of the period.

The demand for virgins was so great that many of the prostitutes were young children. Parliament finally had to pass a law forbidding girls to become prostitutes under the age of thirteen. There's an account of one man who seduced 70 girls in a year, trying desperately to establish a record for 100. Counterfeiting virginity became a major occupation for the medical profession. Books were published on the various techniques. According to Mrs. Hayes' records, a girl could be palmed off as a virgin five or six times, but after that trickery was necessary.

In *Fanny Hill*, there's a description of a special bed designed to help maintain this illusion. Apparently such beds were a standard article of furniture in most brothels. A drawer, operated by a secret spring, was set into the bedpost and inside was a sponge soaked with blood. The girl managed to get hold of this sponge at a crucial moment and give the illusion that her maidenhead had been broken. Fanny also speaks of another technique but warns that if the man insists on the girl's taking a hot bath, this device is revealed. The entire business became so involved that the accounts read like medical journals rather than orgies of lust.

So many references have been made to *Fanny Hill* that something should be said about this curious work. It was written by John Cleland, a British Consular official, who was deep in debt and wrote the book to make money—then, as now, sex being the best paying subject for literature. Cleland certainly knew his subject for the book is a treatise on both normal and abnormal sexual behavior. It also gives an excellent general picture of the times. The plot is much the same as Katharine Winsor's "Forever Amber."

Fanny is a fifteen-year-old country girl whose parents have both died during a smallpox epidemic, a common occurrence in those times. She meets an older girl from London who has come to the country for a visit and is greatly impressed by the girl's lace cap, scoured satin gown, and tawdry ribbons. When the girl returns to London, Fanny goes with her, innocently paying the travel expenses for both of them. The friend then deserts her and Fanny is left on her own.

Fanny goes to an Intelligence Office, a sort of government-sponsored employment agency. The interview costs her a shilling; the woman running the office refusing to give the girl any information until the fee is paid. The woman then tells her, "There are very few places but I will let you know if anything should turn up." Fanny, who has almost no money left, is friendless and desperate.

Sitting in a corner of the Intelligence Office is a friendly, older woman who introduces herself as "Mrs. Brown." She begins to chat with Fanny and then explains that she had come to the office to engage a maid. Fanny is delighted. Only later does she discover that Mrs. Brown pays the woman in the office a small fee to discourage young girls from trying to get honest work.

Fanny goes with Mrs. Brown to her home. At first, everything seems perfect. She is offered a good wage, the servants praise Mrs. Brown as the kindest and best of mistresses and Fanny is told that she is to be more of a "companion" than a maid. Mrs. Brown has several other young girls staying in the house, who are introduced to Fanny as nieces or cousins. Fanny is to share a bed with one of them. The "cousin" turns out to be a Lesbian, but the country girl, puzzled and frightened, does not like to protest to kind Mrs. Brown.

Mrs. Brown now sells Fanny's virginity to an old lecher. The arrangement is that the man will pay 50 guineas for the right to make advances to the girl and another 100 if he is successful. The entire household now go to work on Fanny to encourage her to yield, explaining that the old roué is enormously rich and will marry her if she proves to be satisfactory. However, Fanny cannot stand his advances and puts up a fierce resistance. He prides himself on being irresistible to women, although he is virtually impotent and is forced continually to change girls as the only way of encouraging his flagging powers. Fanny's resistance and his own inability to handle the frantic child drive him mad with shame. When the household is finally forced to interfere, Fanny has a bloody nose and a black eye, and her clothes are half torn off. Even Mrs. Brown decides that this is going too far and she throws the old man out of the house, although keeping his 50 guineas.

A few days later, Fanny comes downstairs to find a handsome eighteen-year-old young buck sleeping off his liquor in the drawing room. He passed out early in the evening and his companions left him on the floor while they went upstairs with the girls. Fanny runs off with this young man, who sets her up in an apartment. Later, his father sends him to manage a factory belonging to the family in the South Seas and Fanny is left penniless and pregnant. She is forced to take another lover and from then on meets one man after another, each representing a different walk of life or another sexual technique. Eventually, Fanny's lover returns from the South Seas. It turns out that Fanny, in spite of all her adventures, has always loved him and the young man loves her. They marry and live happily ever afterwards, Fanny having been left a large sum of money by one of her admirers to whom she was more nurse than mistress.

I've told the first part of this famous book at some length as it gives a good idea of these girls and their backgrounds. It was young girls like Fanny Hill who made up a large part of the "nuns." It would be interesting to know the reaction of one of these children to her first night in the caves—meeting the robed monks, being ferried across the River Styx, and then being raped in the Inner Temple. It's amazing that they kept their sanity. Probably a number of them didn't.

In 1772, Franklin came to England with the illegitimate son of his illegitimate son acting as his secretary. Franklin intended to make one last desperate attempt to convince influential Englishmen that unless the American Colonists' demands were met there would be a revolution in America. Having corresponded with Dashwood, he went at once to West Wycombe.

Franklin and Dashwood got along well. Franklin wrote, "I am in the house as much at my ease as if it were my own; and the gardens are a paradise. But a pleasanter thing is the kind countenance, the facetious and very intelligent conversation of mine host who, having been for many years engaged in public affairs, seen all parts of Europe, and kept the best company in the world, is himself the best [company] existing."

Franklin had been snubbed by most of the English nobility, being as one gentleman remarked, "An almanack maker, a quack, a chimney-doctor (referring to Franklin's invention of the Franklin stove), a soap boiler, a printer's devil, a deist, and the father of several children born out of wedlock." Sir Francis naturally did not object to Franklin's morals, and whatever the Lord le Despencer's shortcomings may have been, he was no snob. Franklin was a brilliant and amusing companion, which was all Sir Francis required of any man. Besides, the Lord le Despencer was interested in the problem of the restless American Colonials. Sir Francis was always sympathetic with rebels and willing to help them.

Since the secretary of the Hell-Fire Club burned the club's records the day before his death, there is no absolute proof that Franklin (or anyone else for that matter) was a member. But we do know that he paid constant visits to West Wycombe and in July 1772 made a special trip from London to spend sixteen days with Sir Francis. We also know that there was a meeting of the club during this period and there seems to be no reason why Franklin should have gone to Wycombe at this special time unless he was a member. Only club members were allowed at Wycombe during club meetings. Franklin did go into the caves, and only club members (except for servants and the "nuns") were allowed past the iron gate. Franklin wrote to a friend in Philadelphia: "The exquisite sense of classical design, charmingly reproduced by the Lord le Despencer at West Wycombe, whimsical and puzzling as it may sometimes be in its imagery, is as evident below the earth as above it." This can refer only to the caves.

Under the circumstances, Franklin would have been shortsighted if he hadn't joined the club. He was a diplomat trying to help his country and the club gave him the entree to some of the most influential men in England.

Franklin was not only a brilliant politician but also an outstanding scientist. In addition, he was a quick thinker. Like Wilkes, he was never led away by the club but was able to keep his head and use the members for his own purpose. During an orgy in the Banqueting Room, the members were kidding Franklin about the "backward Colonists." Franklin assumed a solemn expression and assured the club that the Americans possessed amazing powers—in fact, were adept at magical arts which they had learned from the Indian medicine men. This was just the sort of story the superstitious rakes were willing to believe, and at once there were demands that Franklin give a demonstration of these strange arts.

Franklin gravely rose and taking his cane led the way to the underground river Styx which bubbled and foamed under the lighted torches. Franklin muttered impressive incantations and waved his cane like a magician's wand over the maelstrom. Suddenly the waters became calm.

"A pox on it! If you Yankees can do tricks like that, we will indeed have to take you more seriously," exclaimed Dashwood, half-frightened and half-amused.

Not for many years later did Franklin reveal that as a scientist he was interested in the soothing effects of oil on water. He had had a hollow cane which he filled with oil and occasionally might experiment on any small body of water which he encountered on his walks. He had just returned from a stroll in the country in time to attend the club meeting in the cave and had the cane with him.

Dashwood did everything possible to help Franklin effect some sort of a compromise with the King's Friends. He had Lord North, then the prime minister, down to Wycombe to meet Franklin. He also brought down Bute and Sandwich. None of these men would listen to any of Franklin's arguments. They merely delivered tirades against the American Colonists and told Franklin: "Troops will decide the issue." Then they lapsed into angry silence. Franklin wrote unhappily: "Afterwards we dined, supped, and break-fasted without exchanging three sentences." As fellow club members, Bute and Sandwich saw Franklin several times, and probably he even joined them in the drinking bouts given in the underground Banqueting Hall, but they continued to ignore him.

After a while, Franklin got tired of this silent treatment and decided to give the arrogant lords a little surprise. He wrote a short squib purporting to be a proclamation by Frederick the Great of Prussia. In it, Frederick announced that since the British Isles were originally Saxon colonies, Frederick has decided to tax them. As the English are only colonists, they can not be allowed any say in how they are to be taxed, and, if they protest, Frederick is prepared to use troops to put down the insurrection. Frederick then goes on to outline his plans for raising revenue, which were a burlesque on the tax plans of Lord North and Bute. Frederick concludes that he does not need to worry about the English Navy, as Sandwich has gotten it into such a mess that England can be conquered by a fleet of rowboats.

Franklin got this letter published in a local paper as an actual edict proclaimed by Frederick. He knew that Paul Whitehead, the club's secretary, subscribed to all the papers and every morning would go through them for items of interest to the members. Franklin describes what happened when the paper arrived:

"Whitehead had the papers in another room and we were chatting in the breakfast parlor when he came in to us out of breath with the paper in his hand. 'Here,' said he 'here's news for ye! Here's the King of Prussia claiming a right to this kingdom!' All stared, and I as much as anybody; and he went on to read it. When he had read two or three paragraphs, a gentleman present said 'Damn his impudence; I dare say we shall hear by next post that he is upon the march with one hundred thousand men to back this.' Whitehead, who is very shrewd, soon after began to smoke it and looking in my face said, 'I'll be hanged if this is not some of your American jokes upon us.' "

Most of the members burst out laughing and declared it a fair hit, but Sandwich, Lord North, and Bute weren't amused.

The members had another use for the papers besides obtaining the news. They amused themselves by reading the lines straight across the page instead of down the columns. Some of the better results were recorded:

"This morning the Right Hon. the Speaker . . . was convicted of keeping a disorderly house."

"This day His Majesty will go in state to . . . 15 notorious common prostitutes."

A curious result of Franklin's membership in the Hell-Fire Club was the publication of the *Franklin Prayer Book* which became the basis of the *Book of Common Prayer* still used in most American Protestant Churches today.

The two men were sitting before a fire in West Wycombe House, discussing religion. Both agreed that the current prayer book was intolerably long and dull and as well contained many passages that no intelligent man could believe. They resolved, as Sir Francis later wrote, "to prevent the old and faithful from freezing to death through long ceremonies in cold churches, to make the services so short as to attract the young and lively, and relieve the well-disposed from the inflection of interminable prayers." With this noble end in view, they set to work on the prayer book.

All references to the sacraments and to the divinity of Christ were struck out as well as the Apostles' Creed. Also omitted were the commandments in the catechism and much of the Te Deum. The two men tried to create a book that would answer two questions. What is man's duty to God and what is his duty to his fellow men?

It's a little unusual to find a Satanist and a deist (a man who believes in God but admits of no formal type of worship) engaged in writing prayer books, but the two men were sincere enough. At that time, most established churches presented humanity with one or two choices: Either you believe in the divine right of kings, the unqualified rule of the upperclasses, and the unquestioned authority of the church, or else you are an infidel. Confronted by a choice like that, thousands of intelligent men retorted, "All right, then I'm an infidel." Paradoxical to his behavior Dashwood was basically a deeply religious man. Franklin had made a careful study of religion and had written scores of essays on the subject. His conclusion that "One ought to imitate Jesus and Socrates" might not be orthodox but it shows a sincere desire to find a workable ethical code. Although few people would go along with Franklin on many of his religious ideas, he did present religion in terms of a clear, concise moral duty rather than a long series of involved theological statements expressed in pseudo-legalistic language.

The prayer book was published in England as having been written by the Lord le Despencer who "held in the highest veneration the doctrines of Jesus Christ." But Franklin's share in the book soon became known and the prayer book was always referred to in England as the "Franklin-Despencer Prayer Book." The Church of England turned it down cold, feeling, as one bishop indignantly remarked, "The precious pair should not interfere in religious matters." But in America the book was received with enthusiasm and the entire work was attributed to Franklin.

6 One would have thought that as Wilkes was officially declared an outlaw and could be arrested or shot on sight by any public-minded citizen, the least he could do was to stay out of sight—preferably in the Inner Temple with the boat pulled up on his side of the River Styx. Instead, he proceeded to run for Parliament. With the hearty support of Dashwood and a few more of his old cronies, he bought a small strip of land in Middlesex, thus becoming a citizen of the borough and qualified to represent it in Parliament.

Wilkes' announcement that he would be a candidate for Parliament touched off a series of spectacular demonstrations. Franklin wrote: "I went last week to Winchester and observed that for fifteen miles out of town there was scarce a door or a window-shutter next to the road unmarked with 'No. 45' or 'Wilkes and Liberty,' and this continued here and there to Winchester which is 64 miles. London was illuminated for two nights at the command of the mob who made their rounds at intervals during the whole night and obliged those who had extinguished the candles to light them again, their windows being smashed if they refused." So many candles were lighted that Franklin computed the total cost must have been close to 50,000 pounds.

George III was terrified. He spoke angrily of "that devil Wilkes" and told his supporters that if Wilkes were elected, the monarchy and the power of the King's Friends was in dire peril. He was afraid to go to sleep at night and sat up staring at the illuminated city, constantly asking if his guards were ready to repel an attack. In Franklin's opinion, "If the king had a bad character and Wilkes a good one, George III would have been turned off his throne." But whatever the mob might feel, Wilkes' Hell-Fire Club record stood against him with the more solid element of the country.

Wilkes' power over the London mob was amazing. He had become the symbol of liberty and was almost worshipped as a God. In London antique shops it is still possible to buy porcelain jugs, china statuary, miniatures, and snuff boxes bearing the magic motto "No. 45" or "Wilkes and

Liberty." His quick wit also delighted the crowd. While addressing a street gathering, he noticed a dignified-looking gentleman glaring at him. Wilkes said courteously, "And you, sir, can I count on your vote?"

"I'd rather vote for the devil!" roared the respectable gentleman.

"Certainly. But if your friend doesn't run, can I count on your vote then?"

On another occasion while urging people to vote against the king and the King's Friends, a man angrily shouted, "If I forget my king, may God forget me!"

"I assure you that He'll see you damned first," Wilkes promised him.

There are few records of Wilkes ever having been beaten in these exchanges but he told a couple of stories on himself. Many inns were named after him and his face often appeared on the signs. One old lady stopped him and pointing to a sign with her cane shouted, "There you hang, sir! Everywhere but where you should!" While he was renting a house in London, a pretty little maid showed him around. Wilkes slipped an arm around her waist and whispered, "My pretty dear, are you to be let with the house?" Removing his arm, the girl said severely, "No sir, I'm to be let alone."

Wilkes' most famous sally has passed in our language as a common phrase. At a party, he was offered a pinch of snuff. Wilkes refused it, remarking, "I have no minor vices."

He also coined another conventional expression. Listening to a sycophant sing the praises of some great lord, Wilkes said contemptuously, "Good Lord, man, you lay it on with a trowel!"

It seems doubtful if the mob had much conception of the issues involved except that Wilkes was somehow opposing the hated king and the arrogant King's Friends. George Selwyn amused himself by asking people who were chalking "45" on doors and shutters what the numbers meant. None of the crowd had any idea.

Wilkes had few illusions about the mob. He despised the people who supported him. He was once asked his opinion of a certain man. Wilkes replied contemptuously. "I think little of him. He is a Wilkite, which I never was." On another occasion he was told that one of his supporters had turned his coat and gone over to the opposition. "Impossible! None of my supporters has a coat to turn," retorted Wilkes.

The King was understandably furious that a man condemned as an outlaw should openly walk the streets of London and even run for Parliament. He sent a furious letter to his secretary, Lord Weymouth: "It is absolutely necessary that the utmost be done to seize him. I cannot conclude without expressing my sorrow that so mean a set of men as the sheriff's officers can, either from timidity or interestedness, frustrate a due execution of the law. If he is not soon secured, I wish you would inquire whether there is no legal method of quickening the zeal of the sheriffs themselves."

But Wilkes was so popular that no one dared to move against him. He had petitioned several times to have the sentence of outlawry removed but to no avail. He now demanded to be arrested as a way of forcing the King's hand. As no one would arrest him, Wilkes finally put himself at the head of a mob and marched on the King's Bench Prison where he beat on the door demanding admittance. The frightened warden was forced to let him in and Wilkes established himself in a large, comfortable cell and proceeded to live the life of Reilly, throwing big dinner parties for his friends and writing endless speeches about his "martyrdom."

While resting in prison, Wilkes continued to intrigue against the King and the King's Friends. Due to Franklin's gentle prodding, Wilkes became the great English spokesman for the colonists. He corresponded with John Hancock, Adams, James Otis, and other American leaders who were eager to have him put their grievances before the British government. In the British Museum is a letter to Wilkes from the Sons of Liberty warning him that trouble would soon start in America and begging him to continue his campaign against the King. Wilkes' stand against the government had an enormous effect on the American Colonial leaders. The historian Rough even wrote: "The reasoning used in relation to the Middlesex election and the sentiments naturally awakened are asserted to have occasioned the American War." John Gorham Palfry, the revolutionary leader, announced: "The fate of Wilkes and America must stand or fall together." The Americans didn't seem to have been troubled by Wilkes' shady reputation. Benjamin Kent, one of the Sons of Liberty, wrote him good-naturedly, "I have not seen the *Essay on Woman* but if I should find anything too luscious, I am well fortified by sixty cold North American winters which have hoar'd my head."

Wilkes wrote in reply that as soon as he could get out of jail he would devote a large part of his time to helping the American cause. He urged the colonists not to fight ... he could handle both the king and the King's Friends. He did issue a number of pamphlets defending the colonists— probably as much to annoy the King as because of any real sympathy with the Americans—and soon became the colonist's most popular Englishman. Thousands of babies from Maine to South Carolina were named "John Wilkes Smith" or "Wilkes Jones." Wilkes county in North Carolina was named after him, with Wilkesboro as its principal town. Wilkes-Barre, Pennsylvania, was founded in 1769 and this community also owes its name to the notorious hell-rake. The South Carolina legislature was so moved by his misfortunes that they sent 1,500 pounds to pay his debts at the wineshops and bagnios. However, this thoughtful act only made Wilkes furious. "Why didn't they give me the money instead of wasting it on whores and tradesmen?" he fumed. "Those Colonists will never learn to behave like gentlemen." However, the Carolinians also sent him several hogsheads of prime tobacco for a personal gift to while away the time in prison, and as Wilkes was a great smoker he forgave them for wasting the 1,500 pounds.

Wilkes was also conspiring with the Chevalier d'Eon, that curious gentleman of indeterminate sex, against the British government. You'll recall that the Chevalier was a member of the club and had been examined at the abbey by a committee of matrons to determine his sex. The ladies couldn't make up their minds what he was. It was also the Chevalier who had brought a fellow Frenchman to the caves and the guest ended up by eloping with "Sister Agnes."

The Chevalier was born in Burgundy in 1728 and even from his birth nobody seems to have been able to decide whether he was a boy or girl. He was baptized as boy but was given a girl's name (Genevieve) and was dressed as a girl until he was three years old. Then he was switched over to being a boy again. He attended military school and became an expert swordsman. At the age of 27, the Chevalier was sent to Russia as an undercover agent for Louis XV of France. The King's mistress, Madam Pompadour, was a great friend of the Chevalier's and he owed his appointment largely to her.

The Chevalier dressed as a woman while he was in Russia, partly to avoid suspicion, as no one would believe that a pretty young girl was an expert in military matters and partly because being a woman gave him the entree to the queen. D'Eon obtained a lot of top secret information which he passed on to Madam Pompadour. She, in turn, used the information in any way that would best help her with the King and the King's ministers. Madam Pompadour was always in danger of being kicked out in favour of younger and prettier rivals, and controlling state secrets was one of the ways she used to keep herself on top.

The Chevalier ran up a pretty good record in Russia and was then sent to England to arrange the Peace of Paris. It was largely due to his influence that the terms of the peace were so favorable to France. The Chevalier was a sensation in England. He was asked everywhere and the betting as to his sex ran into thousands of pounds. He dressed as a man but the report of his adventures in Russia had preceded him and he was generally regarded as a woman. But no one really knew. Women tried to seduce him and husbands even urged their wives to make a play for the Chevalier so they would have inside knowledge of his sex and could place their bets accordingly, but the Chevalier played hard to get.

So many attempts were made by drunks and gangs of rowdies to undress the Chevalier that he finally issued a declaration that he was definitely a man, and, if anyone doubted him, he would gladly prove his masculinity on the dueling field. As the Chevalier was a famous swordsman, no one cared to accept his invitation. Just to make sure, the Chevalier made the rounds of all the fashionable clubs with sword by his side, asking if anyone wished to make a test of his virility. He even went up to a few gentlemen who had been particularly outspoken on the subject and slapped them in the face. No one dared to call him out.

However, doubts as to his sex continued. He had a slender, graceful build, and hair never grew on his face or arms. When a German princess was visiting England, she allowed the Chevalier to enter her bedroom while she was dressing. He even attached himself to the princess' suite as a maid of honor during her tour. Little things like this kept people guessing.

About one subject there could be no doubt. The Chevalier was an agent of the King of France. The Chevalier tried to talk Bute into supporting Bonnie Prince Charlie, the Young Pretender, against the King. The two men talked the matter over during many Hell-Fire meetings, but Bute at last decided against it only because "Men and matters are not sufficiently matured." This was hardly a very patriotic attitude for one of the King's Friends to take but is a good example of the standards of the times.

The Chevalier did everything he could to supply Wilkes with funds and Wilkes gratefully accepted his help. D'Eon wrote Louis XV, "Don't you want a riot at the opening of

Parliament? If so, I must have more money for Wilkes and for the others. Wilkes costs us very dearly but the English have Paoli (the Corsican patriot whom the English were subsidizing to cause trouble for the French) whom they support as a bomb in our midst. We need bomb for bomb."

Unfortunately for the Chevalier, Madam Pompadour had died and Louis' new mistress, Madam du Barry, didn't like the hermaphrodite. She censored the letters he sent the king and on several occasions prevented important officials from getting in touch with the Chevalier at critical moments. The King became suspicious of him and as French politics were hopelessly involved D'Eon tried to stay in with everybody. As usually happens in such cases, he succeeded only in antagonizing everybody.

Wilkes, however, didn't need the Chevalier's help—all he needed was the King, who could be relied upon to do the wrong thing at the wrong time. Crowds gathered daily under Wilkes' cell, shouting slogans and tacking up protests while Wilkes harangued them from his window. To break up these demonstrations, the King decided to station a company of troops under the window. Naturally, the troops were attacked. The most aggressive member of the mob was a young man wearing a red waistcoat, who kept stoning the soldiers and yelling insults. Finally, an ensign took three men and started after him. The agitator ran down an alley and disappeared, but the soldiers broke into an outhouse and there on the seat was a young man wearing a red waist-coat. The soldiers promptly shot him. It then turned out that he was the son of a local tradesman and had had nothing whatsoever to do with the riots. While the ensign was trying to get out of this mess, the furious mob charged the troops stationed under Wilkes' cell. The troops fired and killed six people, several of whom were women.

This "massacre," as Wilkes hastened to call it, aroused the whole country. Crowds marched on London demanding Wilkes' release. The angry King positively refused to repeal the act of outlawry against Wilkes, but the situation had now grown so critical that some action had to be taken immediately. The King's Friends went into a huddle and came up with one of the nicest legal quibbles of all time. They announced that the act of outlawry was invalid as it read "at the County Court for the County of Middlesex" and should have been "at the County Court for the County of Middlesex for the County of Middlesex." So Wilkes had never been outlawed after all. Wilkes left the prison sur-rounded by cheering mobs.

To celebrate his triumph, Wilkes went to see his dear friend Sir Francis and the others at West Wycombe. He spent many happy hours ducking the nuns in the Styx as well as discussing the political situation in the colonies with Ben-jamin Franklin. Dashwood had built a handsome and most unusual church called St. Lawrence's on the hill above the caves, nicely designed to fill in a bare spot in the vista as viewed from the front porch of Wycombe Hall. Wilkes duly admired the church. "Some churches have been built for devotion, others from a parade of vanity, but I believe this is the first church which has ever been built for a prospect [scene]," he remarked. "There is only one question I wish to ask—where do you keep the liquor and the girls?"

Dashwood was able to answer the first of the questions immediately. On top of the church a hundred feet from the ground he had constructed a huge ball, some twenty feet in diameter, painted gold. The ball was hollow and could be reached by a ladder from the church tower. Inside were seats and once the door leading into the ball was locked the revellers inside could be as certain of being undisturbed as though they were in the Inner Temple of the caves.

"This is the best Globe Tavern I was ever in!" roared Wilkes as he sat in the ball drinking the "divine milk punch" which was a specialty of the house. "It was a happy thought, Francis, to build a church on top of a mountain for the benefit of the people in the valley below."

The church itself was, and still is, a beautiful if some-what bizarre structure. Sir Francis never allowed his love of the grotesque to interfere with his artistic sense—as West Wycombe Hall and the gardens prove. The Baron le Despencer was interested in oriental art and there is a suggestion of St. Sophia's in Constantinople embodied in the

Moorish arches and great carved pillars. The painted ceilings, and elaborate plaster designs are not generally found in English churches and either by accident or design the stained glass windows are set in such a way that during the long English twilight the entire interior of the church flushes a deep red, much as, witnesses say, the interior of the abbey chapel at Medmenham glowed red from the tinted lamps. On the font is carved the design from the old Rosicrucian lamp which Sir Francis originally got from the George and Vulture and which he took with him first to the abbey and then to the Banqueting Hall in the caves. It shows a snake pursuing doves, an unusual Christian symbol, although the sexton who shows you through the church explains that the snake is meant to represent Evil and the doves Purity. A painting of the Last Supper covers the ceiling of the chancel. The dominant figure is not Christ but Judas. He alone of all the group is pictured looking directly at the viewer, and so no matter where you go Judas is watching you. The effect is rather spooky. It is said that Borgnis, who painted the picture, used Sir Francis as a model for Judas.

There has been a lot of discussion why Sir Francis went to the trouble and expense to build St. Lawrence's. (The church organ alone cost him $30,000.) Some people think he did it as a cover-up for his misdeeds. Others, like Wilkes, think he did it merely to improve the view from West Wycombe Hall. Others think he did it as a very elaborate practical joke and tried to find all sorts of pornographic embolism in the design. As was said before, perhaps Sir Francis was basically a deeply devout man and had a desperate desire for religion. St. Lawrence's was a more conventional manner of displaying that desire than the Medmenham abbey or the Hell-Fire Caves, but fundamentally they were all part of his desire to erect some structure that would help him gain a better knowledge of the mysterious forces that control our lives.

Ben Franklin was in West Wycombe at the time and must have often attended services at St. Lawrence together with the other members of the Hell-Fire Club. As far as Franklin's religious views went, there wasn't too much to distinguish him from Dashwood, although one man has come down to us as a monster of moral depravity and the other as a model of dignified behavior.

Wilkes wasn't able to stay long at West Wycombe, for the elections were coming up. The King's Friends put up as their candidate a nondescript man named Dingley who ran a sawmill and seems always to have been referred to as that "miserable Dingley" by both his supporters and the Wilkites.

Poor Dingley never had a chance. He wrote a letter to Lord Chatham complaining that when he tried to address the crowd, he was attacked by Wilkes' lawyer. Dingley hit him and "got such a hurt from his teeth as to make my right hand very lame and useless." The lawyer knocked Dingley down, telling him, "If you want charge for that blow, go to the treasury to collect it." Dingley then tried to get onto a platform to make his speech, but "The timidity was so epidemic that there was not one of my own party to attend me; instead, I found myself surrounded by 300 or 400 Wilkites who all bore upon me to prevent my getting to offer myself as a candidate." Dingley admitted that the King's Friends had done what they could for him, even to hiring a bunch of Irish chairmen to attack the Wilkites. These chairmen carried the heavy sedan chairs in which elegant ladies and gentlemen traveled around town and were all tough, powerful men. Armed with shillelaghs, the Irishmen tried to keep Wilkites from getting near the polls and did such a conscientious job that they killed one man. But the Wilkites overran the chairmen and carried off the polling boxes, not allowing anyone to vote who didn't have a paper in his hat reading "Wilkes and Liberty." Altogether, it seems to have been a very lively election.

Poor old Dingley died—either from blows he had received from the enthusiastic Wilkites or, as the King's Friends insisted, from a broken heart at his unpopularity. The government forces searched wildly for a candidate who could hold his own against Wilkes and finally came up with a Colonel Luttrell, an Irishman who could have held his own against a herd of man-eating Bengal tigers.

The Colonel came of a distinguished and striking family.

Junius, a popular satirist of the day, remarked: "As far as their history has been known, the son has regularly improved upon the vices of his father and has taken care to transmit them, pure and undiminished, into the bosom of his successor." The Colonel's sister, Lady Elizabeth, ran through a fortune at cards and was thrown in jail for debt. There she met a hairdresser who for 50 pounds agreed to marry her, thus assuming her debts. Lady Elizabeth (she called herself "Princess Elizabeth," as she had been the mistress of the Prince of Wales) fled to Germany where she was arrested as a pickpocket. She spent the rest of her life chained to a wheelbarrow, collecting what was politely called "night-soil"—the contents of chamber pots which were emptied into the streets every morning.

The Colonel had another sister named Mrs. Horton (not to be confused with the Mrs. Horton who was the mistress of the Duke of Grafton and used to boast that she had earned 100 *single* guineas from gentlemen in one day). Mainly as a joke at the expense of Colonel Luttrell, Wilkes is said to have introduced Mrs. Horton to a Hell-Fire meeting as one of the nuns. There she met the Duke of Cumberland who afterward married her—"the weakest act of one who was always considered a very weak man," as Walpole observes. The Duke and Duchess managed to obtain a considerable influence over the young Prince of Wales (later George IV) and educated him in all the excesses which later caused such scandal. Walpole moaned: "So fatal is this man Wilkes to the Crown! Such triumphs start up for him even when he is at the lowest!"

To ridicule Colonel Luttrell, Wilkes managed to get another Irish to run in the elections. He was called "Tiger" Roach and known as "The Terror of Dublin." Arthur Murphy gives the following description of him:

"He used to sit at a table all alone with a half-starved look, a black patch upon his cheek, pale with the idea of murder, a quivering lip and a downcast eye. His soliloquy, interrupted now and then with faint attempts to throw off a little saliva, was to the following effect: 'Hut! a mercer's 'prentice with a bag-wig! Damn my soul if I would not skiver a dozen of them like larks! I'll cudgel him back, breast, and belly for three skips of a louse. Here, you, damn my soul, what do you do here?' One night he started up and called a Mr. Bagnell out of the room and most heroically stabbed him in the dark, the other having no weapon to defend himself with."

Between the "Terror of Dublin," Colonel Luttrell, Princess Elizabeth (who was still in England at the time), Mrs. Horton, and Wilkes, it was a gay election. The Wilkite mobs established road blocks around the voting areas and wouldn't let anyone through who didn't yell "Wilkes and Liberty!" Wilkes himself never doubted the outcome or his power over the people. Once he and Colonel Luttrell were standing on a balcony watching a mob cheering for Wilkes and Wilkes asked his rival casually, "Do you suppose that there are more fools or rogues in that assembly?"

Luttrell looked at him sharply: "Suppose I were to tell them what you just said?"

Wilkes said contemptuously, "Why, in that case I would deny it and then order them to tear you to pieces. They'd obey me at once."

Wilkes had a walk-over. The colonel was scheduled to ride to Hyde Park at the head of an army of his friends whose appearance would overawe the mob. Only twenty of his friends cared to make the experiment. They were supposed to meet in the colonel's garden, but the mob was guarding the gates, so they had to climb over the wall. When they started their march, the mob attacked them so savagely that the men were scattered and nearly killed. Colonel Luttrell rode down one of his own friends in his frantic efforts to escape. Finally Wilkes had to organize a relief party and come to their rescue as he didn't want anyone killed—his record was bad enough already.

Wilkes received 1,143 votes against Luttrell's 296. The mob celebrated by getting drunk at Wilkes' expense (even though he provided the cheapest gin possible it cost him 80 pounds) and Wilkes prepared to take his seat in Parliament.

But George III had issued positive orders that Wilkes was not to be seated in Parliament. An assortment of led captains was sent to challenge Wilkes on every possible pretext but Wilkes was on to that trick and refused to fight. He contemptuously told one man, "I refuse to cut the throat of every desperado who is tired of life."

The King's Friends now played their last card. They managed to force a resolution through Parliament refusing to allow Wilkes to be seated on the grounds that he was a traitor, a blasphemer, and a writer of salacious poems. Only two-thirds of these accusations were true, and, as the Duke of Grafton, the current leader among the King's Friends, used to lead the notorious prostitute Nancy Parsons to the head of his table at formal dinners and insist that the guests show her all respect, it was hard to believe that such men were shocked by Wilkes' private life.

Another series of riots resulted from the decision. Lord North was dragged from his carriage and nearly killed. A group of members who made the mistake of staging a demonstration around a large banner reading "No blasphemer" were knocked down. The wheels were torn off their carriages and the windows were broken. The men were dragged through the streets. After considerable legal fuss, Parliament had to back down. This was the second of Wilkes' two great triumphs which are regarded as milestones in the history of British constitutional liberty. His first victory was to establish the principle of freedom of the press through *No. 45*. His second victory came when he was seated in Parliament, thus establishing that any duly elected man could take his place in the highest governing body of Great Britain regardless of the opposition of the King or even of Parliament itself.

Wilkes now came out openly as the champion for the rebellious American Colonists. Apart from delight in annoying the King, he seems to have had no personal motive except that he was genuinely sympathetic with people fighting for their rights. It would seem probable that he was won over to the American cause by Benjamin Franklin during their meetings at West Wycombe. There is no question that it was Franklin who got Dashwood on the Colonists' side. Before Sir Francis met Franklin, he showed no more interest in the fate of Americans than he did in the fate of the Hindus who were being robbed blind by men like Warren Hastings. With the premier baron of Great Britain and the most influential politician of the day on his side, Franklin was reasonably sure that he could make the King and the King's Friends see light.

Wilkes became the English representative for the Sons of Liberty. He wrote constant letters to James Otis, John Hancock, and Josiah Quincy. He introduced a number of crucial reforms: the enfranchisement of the common man, the elimination of the "rotten boroughs" (the small gerrymander areas whose ward heelers were prepared to "sell" them to any ambitious politician), and the protection of individual liberties against the attacks of the wealthy rakes who controlled the government. Although none of these issues directly affected the American Colonists' cause, they had a tremendous bearing on the whole question of popular representation.

It must be remembered that the cause of American independence was fought as much in London as in Boston or Philadelphia. John Adams wrote: "The real American Revolution is a radical change in the principles, opinions, and sentiments of the people." Not only John Wilkes but the whole Hell-Fire Club played an important part in this change. The hell-rakes set the fashion for new ideas. Whatever else may be said about them, they were brilliant men.

Probably through his connections at the Hell-Fire Club, Franklin managed to get hold of a number of letters written by various prominent men in the colonies to the King's Friends. The most important of these letters was written by Governor Hutchinson of Massachusetts, asking for troops to suppress the rebellious colonists. Franklin sent these letters to Adams and Hancock, who at once published them in the American newspapers.

The Hutchinson Letters, as the whole collection came to be called, touched off a series of events that led directly to the American Revolution. Angry mobs demonstrated against Hutchinson and the other letter writers. Adams and Hancock held a hasty conference with the other revolutionary leaders. It was decided that with troops on the way, some act must be committed that would cause an irreparable breach with England. The answer was, the Boston Tea Party.

When news of the Tea Party arrived in London, Franklin was called before the Privy Council. Dashwood went with him as his "second." The Council demanded to know how Franklin had gotten hold of the Hutchinson Letters. Franklin refused to say. Sandwich shouted: "You are one of the bitterest and most mischievous enemies this country has ever known." Franklin was deprived of his office as postmaster of the American Colonies and the King's Friends were sent to America to get the originals of the letters preparatory to having him tried for high treason.

With Dashwood's help, Franklin arranged a meeting with the aged William Pitt. Pitt was a dying man, but he agreed to make a last appeal before Parliament on behalf of the Colonists. Pitt's speech was one of the greatest of his career. At the end, he fell fainting on the floor. So strong was the power of the King's Friends that only one man dared to come forward to help the stricken statesman. That man was "Hell-Fire" Francis.

Franklin was forced to leave the country. Later when asked what he considered to be the primary cause of the failure of his mission, he replied, "Corruption in the English Government." The crucial governmental positions were in the hands of rakes, half-mad degenerates, and complete incompetents. It was impossible to work with such men.

Wilkes continued his struggle to help the Americans. He had left Parliament to become Lord Mayor of London, a position which gave him even greater power. He was outspoken against "The Intolerable Acts" which closed the port of Boston in retaliation for the Tea Party and which stationed troops in Boston. Remembering Franklin's conviction that the British merchants, the commercial class, would be strongly opposed to war, Wilkes got the merchants of Glasgow, Norwich, Liverpool, Manchester, Birmingham, Dublin, and London to sign a petition announcing that "We must prevent all further oppression to our fellow subjects which real purpose is to establish arbitrary power over all America."

As the British commercial class paid the taxes and could at any time paralyze the government, "such opposition was both efficacious and terrible," as the *Annual Register* reported. Headed by Wilkes, a delegation of wealthy merchants waited on the King to present their petition. The King refused to see them, but, as Wilkes pointed out in speech after speech in Parliament, according to the British Constitution, His Majesty had to receive any petition from his subjects. George III was put in a serious predicament. If he received the petition, he would openly have to refuse a request (it was virtually a demand) made by all the leading businessmen of the country. If he yielded, it meant backing down from the stand he had taken after the Tea Party. He had said, "The Americans will be lions only as long as we are lambs," and he meant to see the Bostonians punished.

By one device or another, George managed to avoid receiving the petition until the spring of 1775. Then, unable to stand Wilkes' heckling any longer, he agreed to meet the delegation. Lord Weymouth, the King's secretary, pompously told Wilkes, "His majesty has graciously agreed to receive the petition but he will not speak to you." Wilkes bowed stiffly and said, "Fortunately I did not anticipate that honor."

The petition was at least presented and now the King would be forced to act. The Americans were certain that George would have to yield. The Continental Congress wrote that war could still be averted. The letter, signed by John Hancock, is in the British Museum. Wilkes pulled two more tricks to hasten the King's decision. He raised 500 pounds for beleaguered Boston and refused to allow the Royal Navy's press gangs to operate within the city limits of London. The press gang was a detachment of men under command of an officer empowered to force men into military, or especially naval, service. At once seamen began deserting by the hundreds and flying to the protection of the city. Sandwich, as First Lord of the Admiralty, was furious but helpless.

It was only a matter of days now before the King would be forced to surrender. Then came word of the Battle of

Lexington and of Colonial troops besieging Boston. The war had begun.

Parliament voted to send an army to put down the rebellion. Wilkes protested: "This is a revolution, not a rebellion. Who knows whether in consequence of this day's mad address in a few years the independent Americans may not celebrate the revolution of 1775 as we do the revolution of 1688?"

He was laughed down and the war program went through.

There was still a bare possibility that Wilkes, with Dashwood's money and support and the help of some of the more liberal members of the club, could still save the situation. Wilkes was as usual heavily in debt. He owed over 20,000 pounds and a special society had even been formed to raise enough money to pay off his creditors. The money was raised, but as soon as the society paid off one lot of debts, Wilkes ran up some more, so the group had a life-time job on their hands. Wilkes would have been ruined many times over if it hadn't been for the generosity of Alderman John Barnard, a wealthy merchant and Wilkes' staunchest supporter. Barnard had stuck by Wilkes all the time he was in prison, exiled, and denounced. More important, he had constantly paid off Wilkes' outstanding debts.

Wilkes had always been a great lady's man. During all his political troubles, he had been paying court to Marianne

Charpillon, a famous courtesan who could pick and choose her lovers. His rival for Madam Charpillon's somewhat shopworn affections was the famous Casanova, the greatest lover in all history. Squinting Wilkes apparently didn't have a chance against the great lover, but Wilkes made good his boast that given half an hour's start, he could best at love-making the handsomest man in the world. Madam Charpillon yielded to Wilkes and gave Casanova the gate. Casanova devotes an entire chapter of his Memories to the outrage.

Alderman Barnard, Wilkes' great benefactor, was an elderly gentleman with a pretty young wife. One evening the lady burst into her husband's room weeping hysterically. Her dead daughter had appeared in a dream and ordered her to confess to her husband that she had been having an affair with Wilkes.

Barnard behaved with considerable dignity. He wrote Wilkes that, due to his age, he could not demand the satisfaction of a duel but he thought that Wilkes had behaved in a very scurvy fashion. He offered Wilkes a chance to vindicate himself, but Wilkes said nothing. Mr. Barnard then wrote Wilkes that he was severing all relations with him and also cutting him out of his will.

Wilkes promptly wrote a series of the most abject letters to the man whom he had deceived, promising never to see Mrs. Barnard again and to make all sorts of reparations. He begged Mr. Barnard to remember his noble efforts to help the common people, offered to become a devout church member—in fact, he would do anything Mr. Barnard asked if only Mr. Barnard would put him back in his will. Possibly nothing Wilkes ever did put him in as bad a light as these letters. Barnard withdrew his support and so Wilkes lost his principal source for campaign expenses.

The Hell-Fire Club considered Wilkes' little escapade with Mrs. Barnard hilariously funny. Wilkes, however, was ruined politically. At the next election, the King's Friends put up a respectable, colorless gentleman named Benjamin Hopkins. He was encouraged to dress simply and always appear in public with his devoted family. Mr. Hopkins didn't amount to much but he had no Hell-Fire Club record. He won the election. Wilkes succeeded only in getting an alderman's appointment. He lost all chances of being able to influence Parliament, and the last chance of a reconciliation between the American Colonists and the government was gone.

7 Wilkes still had one powerful friend—the London mob. To them, he could do no wrong. At any time he could summon up a fanatically howling mass of men, women, and children whom even the King dared not face. But if he lost the mob, he was lost indeed.

The London mob of that period was only slightly superior to the Paris mob who a few years later turned France into a shambles and instituted the Reign of Terror. Even the nobility referred to it as "King Mob" for no one dared to stand in its path once it was aroused. It was composed of people who were hardly human and were treated by their superiors as dangerous wild animals. They lived in a maze of twisted streets, stinking alleys, and ruined houses that were continually collapsing. Few of them could as much as sign their names; almost none could read or write. They stank so badly that they were referred to as "the great unwashed" and fashionable gentlemen who had to leave Pall Mall or Vauxhall held scented sachets to their noses so they could stand the stink. When the madam of a bagnio secured one of the wretched young virgins whose maiden-head was to be sold to the rakes of the Hell-Fire Club for 50 pounds, her first act was always to have the girl washed so the madam could see what she looked like.

Only a few of the main thoroughfares of London were paved and then the paving usually consisted of rocks dumped over the mud and filth of the streets. The middle of a street was generally pitted by holes full of water and garbage. Cart wheels and horses' hoofs flung this mire over pedestrians, so people of any standing always traveled by enclosed sedan chair. Even the windows of the chairs had to be kept constantly closed or the muck was thrown in on the passengers. The sides of the houses were plastered with the filth. On either side of a street ran a ditch called "the kennel" which served as gutters. As there were no water-closets or any kind of plumbing, the chamber pots and other refuse were emptied into these kennels. In the commoner districts, the pots were simply emptied out the windows with the cry of "Stand clear!" Every pedestrian tried to keep close to the sides of the houses as some protection against the filth being thrown over him, and savage fights frequently took place over who would "take the wall." In some of the better areas, steppingstones were laid across the street so people could cross without wading through the morass. In most districts there were no street lamps but you could hire linkboys who ran ahead with lighted torches. These boys were frequently in the pay of thieves and after leading their employer into a trap would plunge their torches into the mud and then run, leaving the terrified traveler to be murdered, raped, or robbed.

As one writer remarked, "These people take a rat's-eye view of life." They were infinitely more dangerous than any savage tribe and nearly as ignorant. When the Duke of Wellington was looking over a batch of new recruits he remarked, "I don't know what effect they will have on the enemy, but by God they frighten me!" Press gangs, armed with muskets, clubs, and cutlasses were sent out to round up men for the navy like animal trappers capturing wild beasts. Terrific battles often took place between the slum dwellers and the press, as the men knew what sort of a life awaited them in the navy. Samuel Johnson remarked, "No man who can get into jail would go into the navy, for a ship is a floating prison with the additional chance of being drowned." Discipline was enforced with the cat-o'-nine-tails and a "dozen with the cat" was considered in the nature of a merely mild reprimand. Captain Marryat tells of seeing a man receive five dozen lashes for spitting on the deck. On one ship the captain shouted to the men aloft making sail, "I'll have the last man down flogged!" In their desperate struggle to get down, two men fell and were killed. "Throw the lubbers overboard!" was the captain's only comment.

It was taken for granted that the only way to handle such people was by torture or the hangman's noose. To pick a pocket, steal a sheep, or shoplift an object of over five shillings value were all capital offenses. It was impossible to enter London without passing at least half a dozen gallows with bodies "hanging in chains," put in iron cages to preserve them as long as possible as a warning to evil-doers. On the spikes over Temple Bar gate were still a few rotting heads which nobody had bothered to remove, although the custom of "spiking heads" had been officially abandoned. No one, certainly not the mob, thought of objecting to such practices. "Hanging days" when fifteen or twenty people were executed on Tyburn Hill were regarded as public holidays. Rogers mentions seeing a cart headed for Tyburn full of women and little girls going to be hanged. On such days, all the shops were closed and crowds assembled to watch the hangings. A good seat in the front row could cost as much as a guinea, depending on how well-known the criminal was and how he or she was to die. Some of the executions were especially ghastly:

Eight soldiers who had attacked an officer were first

half-hanged and then cut down while still conscious. Their entrails were cut out and burned in front of them. Women who had killed their husbands (legally a form of treason) were burned alive. One of them was Catherine Hays who gave the executioner a lot of trouble as described in the *Annals of Newgate 1776*:

"She was brought to the stake, was chained thereto with an iron chain running around her waist and under her arms, and a rope around her neck, which was drawn through a hole in the post; then the faggots, light brushwood intermixed with straw being piled all around her, the executioner put the fire thereto in several places, which immediately blazed out. As soon as the same [flames] reached her she with her arms pushed down those [faggots] which were before her, when [and] she appeared in the middle of the flames as low as the waist, upon which the executioner got hold of the end of the cord which was around her neck and pulled it tight in order to strangle her, but the fire soon reached his hand and burned it so that he was obliged to let go again; more faggots were immediately thrown upon her and in about three or four hours she was reduced to ashes."

One woman condemned to be hanged got her revenge on Jack Ketch, the hangman. The clothes of the condemned were part of the hangman's prerequisites. This lady began to undress on the scaffold and throw her clothes to the crowd. To get even, Ketch swore that he'd pull her up and let her strangle slowly to death but the woman fooled him by jumping off and breaking her neck.

George Selwyn, one of the most prominent members of the Hell-Fire Club, never missed a hanging, and when his friends used to make up parties to attend the executions they always included George. One such invitation reads: "Harrington's porter was condemned yesterday. Cadogan and I have already bespoken places at the Brazier's (a house overlooking Tyburn where gentlemen could rent seats at the windows) and I hope Parson Digby will come in time enough to be one of the party. I presume we shall have your honor's company if your stomach is not too squeamish for a single swing." Selwyn got off one of his best wisecracks— or *bon mots* as they were called then—at the beheading of a Scot rebel lord named Lovat. Some women were teasing him afterward and asked him how he could stand seeing a man's head cut off. Selwyn replied with his famous drawl, "Nay, my dear ladies, I made amends for I went to see it sewed on again." He was telling the truth. The dead lord's family had asked to have the head sewed on before he was buried. Selwyn had indeed gone to the undertaker's to watch the operation performed. After it was over, Selwyn caused a burst of laughter by imitating the Lord Chancellor's voice and saying solemnly, "My Lord Lovat, your lordship may now rise."

Many ladies of rank also attended hangings. One old countess wrote a catty letter to a friend about a young debutante who pretended to be so tender-hearted and sentimental that she even cried when watching the execution of criminals. However, some of the cases were so pitiful that even the nobility actually were mildly touched. In 1777, a fourteen-year-old girl was found with some farthings hidden in her corset. She had whitewashed them in the hope that she could pass them off for silver. She was condemned to be burned alive, although she pleaded that her employer had ordered her to try to pass the coins and had beaten her until she consented. She was in the cart starting to Tyburn when Lord Weymouth, the King's secretary, "humanely but casually" (to quote the *Annual Register*) ordered her spared. Her master was hanged instead.

Other prisoners were not so lucky as to be simply hanged. Japhet Cook, who was convicted of forgery, was seated in a chair on a platform where Charing Cross Station now stands. "The hangman, dressed like a butcher, came to him and with a knife like a gardener's pruning knife cut off his ears and with a pair of scissors slit off both his nostrils, all of which Cook bore with great patience; but at the searing with a red-hot iron of his right nostril the pain was so violent that he got up from his chair. His left nostril was not seared so he went down from the platform bleeding." The searing was intended to close the wounds so the man wouldn't bleed to death.

For minor offenses, the accused might only be exposed in the pillory, although in many cases this was virtually equivalent to a death sentence. The pillory was like the stocks except it was on a pole. There were three holes: two for the victim's hands and one for his neck. Once locked in the pillory, he was helpless.

Criers would announce when anyone was going to be exhibited in the pillory and huge crowds would assemble to take part in the sport of baiting the victim. They would come carrying baskets of rotten eggs (the warehouses did quite a trade selling rotten eggs for this purpose), decaying vegetables, mud balls, and even rocks. As soon as the prisoner was safely locked in the pillory, the hangman had to start running to escape the fusillade. So much stuff was thrown that the wealthier prisoners paid the hangman to keep their faces wiped clear of the garbage with a long pole, otherwise they were apt to suffocate. Those who didn't have any money were in a bad way. Matthew Prior in the *Life of Burke* says:

"Two men were punished at the same time for the same offense. One of them, being of short stature and remarkably shortnecked, could not reach the hole made for the admission of the head. The officers of justice nevertheless forced his head through the hole and the poor wretch hung rather than stood. Previous to being put in he had begged for mercy from the mob which they seemed very little willing to bestow. He soon grew black in the face and the blood issued from his nostrils, his eyes, and his ears. The mob nevertheless attacked him with great fury. The officers, seeing the situation, opened the pillory and the poor wretch fell down dead on the stand of the instrument. The other man was likewise so maimed and hurt by what was thrown at him that he lay there without hope of recovery."

Curll, the printer of pornographic books, who provided Dashwood with his first copy of *How to Celebrate the Black Mass*, was pilloried. However, he had enough money to buy off the crowd.

Being put in prison was nearly as bad a fate—unless like Wilkes one had enough money to pay for a suite of rooms and order his own meals. Otherwise, he ran a good chance of being eaten alive by the rats. In the *State of Prisons* report for 1776, there's the following comment about a cell in Knaresborough Gaol:

"(The cell) is under the hall, of difficult access, the door about four feet from the ground. Only one room, about twelve feet square, earth floor, no fireplace, very offensive; a common sewer from the town running through it uncovered. I was informed that an officer confined here took in with him a dog to defend him from the rats; but the dog was soon eaten and the prisoner's face much disfigured by them."

The insane asylums were run on the same principle as

zoos except that the inmates were not protected from the public. "Visiting the madhouses" was a popular sport and one of Hogarth's paintings show two elegantly dressed society ladies wandering through Bedlam amusing themselves by watching the antics of the patients. The basic principle employed in treating psychopathic disorders was to beat it out of the victim. Manacles, whips, blows, kicks, scourgings, and a snake pit into which the patients were lowered to scare them sane were the standard treatments. Tickets of admission were sold for twopence at the door.

A visitor to Bedlam in 1753 wrote: "To gratify the curiosity of a country friend, I accompanied him a few weeks ago to Bedlam. It was in the Easter Week when to my surprise I found a hundred people at least who having paid their twopence apiece were suffered unattended to run up and down the wards making sport and diversion of the miserable inhabitants."

Although the last witch legally convicted in England was Jane Wenham in 1712, the people still believed in witchcraft and were apt to give old ladies a hard time. In the village of Oakley, the local parson became convinced that a sixty-year-old woman was a witch and ordered her thrown into the Ouse River to see if she would float. It was believed that a witch couldn't sink but always floated on the surface of water. If she drowned, she was innocent and everybody felt badly about it. A mob speedily collected and the poor old girl was bound hand and foot and tossed into the river. Sure enough, she floated (probably some air had gotten trapped under her clothes) so she was hauled out and preparations made to burn her alive. The old woman pleaded for mercy and begged to be given another chance. That seemed fair enough to the crowd so they threw her in again. She still floated. This was considered to be conclusive proof of her guilt so she was pulled out a second time and the stake was readied.

The old lady knew that she was finished and lay weeping on the ground, all hope gone. The Bible says, "Thou shalt not suffer a witch to live," a commandment which has probably been responsible for more deaths than any other eight words in history. The parson was busily directing the putting up of the stake and the collection of firewood but luckily for the old woman there were a few skeptics in the crowd and they insisted that she be weighed against the church Bible. A true witch always weighed less than a Bible. Scales were brought and the witch and the Bible were weighed. As the Bible only weighed twelve pounds, the woman outweighed it and in spite of the parson's furious objections, she was turned free.

This story is interesting not only because it shows the mobs' general level of intelligence but because it partially explains why so many intelligent men of the period felt that religion was a menace and that anything they did to ridicule it was a praiseworthy act. When many clergymen were lecherous drunks, like Churchill and Laurence Sterne, and in addition ministers, were urging mobs to burn women for witchcraft, freethinkers were likely to regard religion with suspicion if not with actual hatred.

When they were not burning witches or stoning prisoners the mob amused themselves with bear-baiting, setting dogs on bulls, badger-baiting, and cockfighting. A bear would be chained by the neck in the middle of an open space and dogs would be turned on him. The crowd would bet on the first dog killed, the first dog to take a hold, and the first pair of dogs to get the bear down. Bull-baiting was often referred to as the national amusement. The bulldog, the symbol of the British nation, was developed for this sport. The dog was bred to have an unshot jaw so that even while he was holding the bull by the nose he could still breathe, and a broad, squat body on bandy legs to make it difficult for the bull to turn him over.

When attacked by dogs, an experienced bull kept his head low to protect his nose and present his horns to the pack. If he managed to toss a dog, the dog's owner ran in and tried to catch the animal as it fell to keep its back from being broken. One man stood by with a pole to push the falling dog into the arms of its owner. Once a dog took his hold, nothing could get him loose. Whatever portion of the bull's nose he was holding had to be cut off. Bulls that were veterans of many baitings had no noses ... they had been sliced away piece by piece.

In badger-baiting, the badger was put into a small barrel and the dog had to prove his courage by going into the barrel and dragging the badger out. As a badger can put up a terrific fight, especially in a confined space where the dog can't get him by the back of the neck, this was generally considered the acid test of a good dog. Dogs were also trained to fight each other. As it was thought that courage came through the female line, to test the bravery of a bitch before she was bred she was allowed to lock her teeth in another dog. The breeder then cut off her toes one after another. If in spite of the pain the bitch kept her death-grip, she was considered brave enough for breedings.

Cockfighting was so popular that it was called the "royal diversion." The most famous pit was the Royal Cockpit in St. James' Park. An advertisement for a main read:

"On 12th July 1731 will be seen the royal sport of cock-fighting for two guineas a battle. Tomorrow begins the match for four guineas a battle and 20 guineas the odd battle, and continues all the week, beginning at four o'clock."

The most famous main took place between the birds of Joseph Gilliver and the Earl of Derby. Each man fought seven birds for a stake of 1,000 guineas (about $5,000) a main and 5,000 guineas the match. The match was won by Gilliver, five mains to two.

Prize-fighting was also popular and the men fought until one was beaten unconscious or so blinded that he could no longer go on. One fighter was led out of the ring weeping, "I'm not beat, but what good does that do me when I can no longer see to hit him?" Often fights ran fifty or sixty rounds. A fighter called Buckhorse was so tough that he allowed young gentlemen to amuse themselves by knocking him down, for half a crown a crack. Men were knocked of the ring, their legs broken, fingers broken, or he cracked open, and they still crawled back to continue fight. The managers revived them by spitting brandy in their faces, spraying it through their teeth. Women also fought. On June 22nd 1768:

"Two women fought for a new shift valued at half a guinea. The battle was won by a woman called Bruising Peg, who beat her antagonist in a terrible manner."

It was taken for granted that anyone running for office had to hire a mob to attack his opponent. The following "Bill of Costs" for an election, although meant satirically, gives a good example of the general attitude.

For bespeaking and collecting a mob	20 pounds
For scores of huzza-men	40 pounds
For roarers of the word "Church"	40 pounds
For several gallons of punch on tombstones	30 pounds
For demolishing two houses	200 pounds

For breaking windows	20 pounds
For a set of notorious liars	50 pounds
For payment of fines	30 pounds

George IV asked one man which of two candidates he thought would win. The man answered "The survivor, sire."

In addition to the standard practices listed above, the King would occasionally send the troops to vote against a measure he disliked and ambitious politicians would buy up all the coaches and sedan chairs so no one could get to the polls. Landlords were paid to tell tenants that they would be evicted if a certain man were elected and the opposition voters were often given free drinks—mixed with knockout drops—to make sure that they'd pass out before they could cast their ballots.

The cost of the "rotten boroughs" were openly advertised. To buy County Down cost 60,000 pounds. William Wilberforce, the great opponent of the slave trade, had to pay 8,500 pounds in order to get a seat in Parliament so he could fight the evil. Franklin said, "I can do nothing against such corruption." It was the age of scandal.

There were constant riots. Franklin reported that he saw "riots about corn, riots about elections, riots of colliers, riots of coal-heavers, riots of sawyers, riots of Wilkesites, riots of chairmen, riots of smugglers." The mob was beginning to feel its strength and to realize that the government was helpless against it.

Perhaps the most grotesque of these riots was the "O.P." mania. Although this riot occurred a few years later (in 1808) a brief description here will show how easily the mob could be moved to fighting frenzy by any trivial issue as long as some simple slogan was given them to shout.

The Covent Garden Theater had burned down and had been rebuilt in a more elaborate style. To defray the cost, the management increased the cost of admission by sixpence (about a dime). For some reason difficult to determine, this innocent action infuriated the mob. When the theater reopened, the crowd in the pit (the cheapest seats) began shouting and stamping so the play could not proceed. Some genius raised the war cry of "Old Prices!" and this was quickly shortened to "O.P.!" It was immediately taken up by the mob gathered outside the theater. Within a few hours, the slogan "O.P." had spread throughout London. Raging mobs chalked it on doors and sidewalks. Picket lines were thrown across streets to force everyone who passed to shout "O.P.!" Within a few days, the stores were full of hats with O.P. stamped upon them, O.P. bonnets for ladies, waistcoats with O embroidered on one flap and P on the other, O.P. handkerchiefs and even toothpicks. Flags with O.P. stamped on them were even flown from poles and a new verse added to "God Save the King."

"O Johnny Bull be true,
Confound the prices new

And make them fall!
Curse Kemble's politics,
Frustrate his knavish tricks,
On God our hopes we fix
T' upset them all!"

Kemble was the manager of the theater.

The riots became so bad that the government was forced to appoint a special committee of prominent men to see if the increase of prices was justified. After going over the theater's book, the committee published its report. It stated that the theater's profits were now only $3^1/_2$% and if they returned to the old prices, the theater would lose 15% and be forced to close. This report only provoked fresh outbursts. Mobs marched down the streets chanting "Come forth, O Kemble! Come forth and tremble!" A famous Italian singer, Madam Catalani, who was appearing at the Garden was also attacked by cries of "No Cats! No Catalani!" The uprising became so bad that the Horse Guards had to be called out.

The theater again tried to open, but the mob in the pit was uncontrollable. In the middle of their outcries against Kemble and "Madam Cat," an Irishman jumped and shouted to the crowd to listen to him. "Say what you will about Kemble, but I'll be damned if I'll hear you insult a lady!" he roared. Instead of being beaten to death, the crowd cheered and agreed to leave the Italian prima donna out of the row. Kemble himself came out on the stage and tried to reason with the crowd but he was shouted down.

As always seems to have happened in these riots, a gentleman publicity seeker appeared to lead the crowd. He was a Mr. Clifford, a lawyer, who appeared at the theater wearing a hat with a new emblem—a large O with a small p in the center of it. Clifford attracted so much attention that the distracted police, who were trying to preserve some sort of order, asked him to leave or at least take off his hat. Clifford refused and was dragged off to jail, followed by a howling mob attacking the policemen.

Clifford was tried the next day for instigating a riot. Clifford immediately put the whole situation on a high moral plane. "When an Englishman cannot wear what kind of a hat he likes, our constitutional safeguards are gone and we are no better than slaves!" he shouted. He was acquitted and was carried to his home on the shoulders of the cheering crowd.

From then on Clifford became the leader of the mob. He was soon the most famous man in England. He spent hours every day haranguing the enthusiastic multitude on their constitutional rights and urged them to keep up the fight for the O.P. He was rearrested several times and the mob changed their cry to "Clifford and O.P.!" Finally he was brought to trial and the whole country waited breathless for the verdict of the jury.

Although the Napoleonic wars were in full sway on the continent and the future not only of Great Britain but the entire world hung in the balance, no one cared for anything but the result of the "O.P. trial," as it was called. The jury finally found that Clifford was innocent and awarded him 5 pounds for false arrest. The judge announced: "The country will be lost as a result of this verdict. There is a spirit of a mischievous and destructive nature abroad which threatens awful consequences." The mob, however, was overjoyed. Signs were raised, "A British jury forever," and householders were ordered to keep candles burning all night in their windows to celebrate the victory, on pain of having the glass smashed.

After holding out for nearly three months, the theater finally announced a compromise. The seats in the pit would be kept at the old prices but the box seat prices would be increased to make up for it. The mob hailed this compromise as a victory and dropped the issue. It was just in time, for the situation was fast getting out of control.

Although the O.P. riots were pretty much of a farce, they show the dangerous, unreasonable character of the London mob that could be readily controlled by any demagogue shouting any simple slogan. The mob was desperate and had nothing to lose. The people composing it knew vaguely that they were abused, held in contempt, and exploited. But they were beginning to realize their own strength. This was a deadly combination. In 1780, it led to riots that were far from a joke: the terrible Gordon Riots which destroyed most of London and caused the death of hundreds of people. They also caused the final fall of John Wilkes.

The Hell-Fire Club played its part in causing these riots. There had always been in England an inherent respect for law and order which even the lowest members of the mob acknowledged. There had been respect for the monarchy. There had been respect for religion. People had at least given lip service to the ideals of decency and morality. To the brilliant, half-mad members of the club all these conceptions were nonsense. Worse than nonsense, they were middle-class. They were the standards of the respectable, beef-eating John Bull who knew nothing of art and literature and whose outlook was bound by a set of stereotyped conventions. The club had set out to ridicule and destroy these conventions. To a large extent, they had succeeded.

8 The club had prided itself on not being bound by the rules that governed ordinary people. They had made fools of two monarchs—George II and George III—and had done much to destroy the popular belief in the "divine right of kings." In so doing, they had paved the way for the American Revolution. They had also paved the way for riots. Brilliant themselves, the club members saw clearly that these kings were heavy-handed, plodding men, and despised them for it. Yet both these kings had been inherently honest and both tried to be fair. The club saw nothing in honesty or fairness except a subject for ridicule. But if Dashwood, Bute, Sandwich, Churchill, and, above all, Wilkes had devoted as much ingenuity and effort to trying to help these not too intelligent monarchs instead of thinking up clever schemes to make them look like fools, much suffering would have been averted. This is perhaps the great trouble with scintillating, witty people. In their contempt for conventionality they ignore the need for something besides frescoes by Italian artists and ingeniously contrived pornographic statues.

Latent antagonism to Roman Catholicism ran as an undercurrent in England of the time. To the intelligentsia of the day, Catholicism with its saints, solemn pageantry, medals, Holy Water, and stories of the miraculous appearance of the Virgin was anathema. The Catholic Church was the favorite butt for the jests of the rakes. When George Selwyn pulled his little stunt of taking a chalice into a bar and asking everyone to take a swig, saying, "Do this in memory of me," he was arrested for blasphemy. He was acquitted when his lawyer pleaded that he had "only been trying to expose the superstitious practices of the Romanist church." To deliver a parody on the Mass, to tell dirty jokes about the Pope, to repeat scandalous stories of the immoral practices of monks and nuns was considered the height of educated humor.

The elaborate Black Mass of the Hell-Fire Club was merely an extreme form of this sort of wit. It had been permitted to continue because the members claimed that they were attacking the Catholic Church rather than religion as a whole. Actually, it is impossible to deliver a vicious attack against any religious group who sincerely believe that they are worshipping God, without attacking religion as a whole and thereby all basic ideas of decency. The Hell-Fire Club had become famous throughout England. It was known that its members consisted of many of the most talented and highly educated men in the country. If the intelligentsia believed that the Catholic Church was so evil that even devil worship was superior, why should the common man doubt their leaders' word?

In 1780, a bill was introduced in Parliament to relieve the English Roman Catholics from a series of various repressive measures which had been on the books for over a hundred years. These measures, forbidding certain civil liberties to Catholics, had not been enforced for a long time but the government wanted them erased from the record once and for all. A small group of rabid clergymen, fanatics, and publicity seekers decided to oppose the bill. Needing a title to make their group look respectable, they selected the 29-year-old nobleman Lord George Gordon, the third son of the Duke of Gordon.

About the most merciful thing that can be said of Lord George is that he was unquestionably half-mad and not responsible for his actions. He was an obscure man who had never done anything one way or another but like so many of his contemporaries he was an exhibitionist and desperately in need of some sort of recognition. He was made honorary head of the collection of screwballs who were opposing the bill and was told to call a mass rally on St. George's field in London for everyone wishing to save the country from the Papists.

Lord George announced the rally but no one turned up except his own small group. Nothing daunted, the group decided to march on the House of Parliament and stage a demonstration there to protest passage of the bill. They started off in fine style and were gradually joined by a long tail of riffraff as they progressed through the streets. So far, they'd had no slogan, but some talented individual raised the cry of "No Popery!" It was instantly taken up by hundreds of voices. Within minutes, crowds poured from the slums of Whitechapel and Seven Dials yelling the new warcry with all the enthusiasm with which they had formerly shouted, "Wilkes and Liberty" and would in a few years be crying "O.P."

By a curious bit of irony, the Duke of Richmond had just risen to place before the house a bill which would have put all power in the hands of the people, because, as the duke said, "We can trust the integrity of the average Englishman." The duke was still speaking when Lord George arrived at the door followed by the frenzied mob. Some of the peers were still entering the house and were promptly attacked. The elderly Lord Bathurst was dragged out of his carriage and kicked into the gutter. Lord Stormont's carriage was torn to pieces and he was only saved from a like fate by a group of his friends. Lord Sheffield later wrote that the Bishop of Lincoln (a Protestant but a man known to be liberal in his views towards Catholics) "only escaped with his life by a miracle." He was throttled until blood ran out of his mouth and his clothes were torn off. He managed to crawl into a house and later had to be smuggled out dressed as a woman. The Bishop of Rochester was told that a cross would be branded on his forehead if he didn't oppose the bill. Lord George stood watching this spectacle with a benign smile on his lips.

Several lords hurried out of the house when they heard the commotion. One exclaimed, "For heaven's sake, Lord George, speak to these unfortunate people and tell them to go home." Lord George's reply was to turn to the mob and ask, "Do you see how I am crossed and attacked at every point?"

The house was forced to adjourn but the mob did not. It roamed the streets yelling its new slogan, "No Popery" and ordering householders to write the magic words on their doors and shutters. Teenagers ran from house to house threatening to chalk up "A Catholic lives here" unless they were given money. One group went to the Sardinian Embassy, broke in and smashed the ambassador's private chapel. They then dragged the altar, crucifixes, and statues into the street and burned them.

As the government did not dare to oppose them, the mob grew steadily worse. The next day they started a systematic looting of Catholic churches. Sacerdotal vestments, ornaments, the beautiful altar pieces, and even the organs were fired. They also attacked the homes of prominent Catholics. Lord Mansfield's house was burned and with it one of the most valuable private libraries in Europe. Sir John Fielding's home was also burned as was Sir George Savile's. The mob then began to burn Protestant churches and the homes of ministers. As always happens in such cases, what had begun as an attack on one religion soon became an attack on all.

The next step was also inevitable. The criminal element took over the mob and began to use it for its own purposes. An assault was made on Newgate Prison where many of the criminals' friends were being held. The mob, armed with crowbars, mattocks, clubs, and even spokes torn from cart wheels, poured down upon the prison doors. A group of watchmen had been drawn up to receive them but the crowd shouted "Papists! Catholic sympathizers!" and the watch was hurriedly withdrawn. No politician or magistrate dared to be labeled as a Catholic sympathizer; it meant political suicide. The mob attacked the prison gates and poured in, setting fire to the place as they did so. The poet Crabbe describes the scene:

"They threw every piece of furniture they could find into

the street, firing them on the instant. I saw Lord George Gordon in a coach drawn by the mob, bowing as he passed along. He is a lively looking young man in appearance and nothing more, though just now he is the popular hero. The prison was a remarkably strong building, but, determined to force it, they broke the gates with crows and climbed up the outside of the cell part. They broke the roof, tore away the rafters, and having got ladders, they descended, flames all around them. The prisoners escaped. You have no conception of the frenzy of the multitude. The doors and windows appeared like the entrances to so many volcanoes."

The next day was afterward known as "Black Wednesday." The mob was in complete control of the city. In hopes of saving their property and their lives, people chalked up "No Popery" on their houses but it did no good. Catholic and Protestant houses alike were sacked and fired. The Italian clown, Grimaldi, hopefully put up a sign "No religion!" and his home was spared. The crowd reached the great Langdale Distillery and looted it. Jesse describes the scene:

"The flames bursting forth in volumes from the distillery were rendered more terribly vivid in consequence of their being fed by the streams of burning spirits. In the fierce glare, men, women, and children were to be seen rushing from their homes, carrying off such articles as they were most anxious to preserve. Pails full of gin were handed about among the crowd. Not only men but women and children were to be seen sucking up gin and other spiritous liquors as they flowed along the kennels. Here and there lay drunken wretches on the ground in a state of insensibility. Some of the rioters while in this state perished in the flames, others literally drank themselves to death."

Business was now entirely suspended. All shops were shut and people were fleeing the city by the thousands. The mob attacked the Artillery Grounds and seized the arms. The troops made an attempt to stop them, but as usual the cry of "Papist supporters!" was enough to cause them to fall back. The Fleet Prison, the King's Bench Prison, the Borough Clink, and Bridewell were attacked and the prisoners were turned loose.

By now, one-third of the city was in flames. The Lord Mayor was quaking in his mansion and even the King was too afraid of being called a Papist to order out the troops. The aldermen did nothing except to order the watch not to interfere with the rioters. Sir Nathaniel Wraxall wrote that during the worst of the riot he saw a watchman with a lantern in his hand walk past a group of people looting a shop, meanwhile calling, "Two o'clock and all's well!" He also mentions that he could read the time by the clock of St. Andrew's church by the light of the flames.

In 1780 (the time of the Gordon riots), the British troops in America had invaded the southern states, captured Charleston, S.C., and were moving north towards the fatal battle of King's Mountain. It was a crucial moment in the war on which the fate of the British Empire depended, yet the London mob were more interested in chalking "No Popery" on walls than in the future of the nation. At a time when the British government was trying to control the American Colonists, they could not even control their own people and prevent the nation's capital from being looted and sacked. Throughout the riots, Sandwich and Lord Bute were staying in the latter's magnificent mansion, Luton Park House, amusing themselves with 50-guinea teenage virgins and a plentiful supply of fine wines while telling each other between hiccups that the American Colonists weren't ready yet for independence.

Wilkes was an alderman, but he too took no action during the first four days of the riots. There was some excuse for Wilkes. Now that he had lost the financial support of Barnard by seducing his wife and was Public Enemy No. 1 as far as the King and the King's Friends were concerned, his only hope was to stay in the good graces of the mob. Other politicians backed by wealth, rank, or influence might dare to defy the people; Wilkes never could. Wilkes had never made any bones about the fact that he was an opportunist ready to do anything that would advance his own interests. He had once remarked, "Accident made me a patriot." It was said of him, "Wilkes has every vice but one: he is not a hypocrite." So no one expected Wilkes to interfere with the rioters. There was only some mild surprise that he had not got on the bandwagon by joining the cry of "No Popery" especially as he was a prominent member of the notoriously antireligious Hell-Fire Club which had been founded to mock Catholicism.

Yet Wilkes was a tortured man during those four days. Whatever his original attitude towards the people may have been, he had become the great spokesman for the rights of the common man. Perhaps he had always believed in the rights of the common man, especially as he had started out in life as one himself. Perhaps he had come to believe his own oratory, as often happens with demagogues. Once during a debate in the House of Commons, he had angrily told his opponent, "Sir, I consider the voice of the people to be the voice of God"—a phrase much used by politicians ever since. Possibly Wilkes had been sincere when he said it. Certainly he had been sincere enough in treating the King and the aristocracy with contempt and had put his faith in the hands of the common man.

Wilkes, more than any other one man, had succeeded in breaking the power of the upper classes and putting that power in the hands of the people. He had taught the mob to use their power in the "No. 45" riots and again in the Middlesex election riots. He had proven to them that the government could not stand against them. They were now using that knowledge in this terrible fashion.

However, Wilkes himself was safe enough. If he wished to advance his political position (and Wilkes always did want just that) he could harangue the crowd together with Lord George. If by any remote chance he didn't want to take advantage of this golden opportunity, he had merely to stand pat. All the rest of the politicians were doing so—even the King.

On the fourth day of the riots, when one-half of London, the world's largest city and the seat of the British Empire, had been destroyed, Wilkes went to see the Lord Mayor of London. The mayor was hiding in his mansion with a big "No Popery!" sign hung over the door and a company of Horse Guards to protect him. He was sweating when he received Wilkes.

"Sir, I wish your permission to call in the troops and put down the riots," Wilkes told him.

The mayor was startled. "Are you mad? It would ruin me politically. I'd be accused of being a secret Catholic. And what about you? You might as well shoot yourself."

"Half of London is gone," replied Wilkes calmly. "We cannot afford to lose the other half. Worse yet, we cannot allow the people to disgrace themselves like this."

"Get out of here!" roared the mayor. "Oppose the common people? What mad idea will you Hell-Fire Club rakes think of next? Besides which, you were always supporting the common man!"

"Oh, I can't really blame them," replied Wilkes. "After all, the mob are my old pupils. Now they've merely set up for themselves."

Although this exact conversation above (except for Wilkes' last speech which he later gave in return to an angry question) is conjecture, something very similar to it did occur. Wilkes did go to the Lord Mayor and was refused the use of troops.

Wilkes still had his colonel's commission in Dashwood's fashionable troop and so had the authority to command militia. He was an alderman and so had the authority to raise a posse (from the legal phrase "posse comitatus," meaning "a committee with powers to take forceful action"). Knowing that to interfere with the riots could mean his own ruin, he waited as long as possible before moving against the mob. On the fifth day of the riots the mob decided to attack and loot the Bank of England. The bank was to 18th Century Great Britain what Fort Knox is to us today—the repository for the national wealth. If it went, the pound sterling would become worthless and the nation would collapse. The proverbial expression "as safe as the Bank of England" would be a joke and the country would be lost.

When Wilkes learned that the rioters were planning to attack the bank, he hurriedly gathered a small force of citizens armed with old muskets, fowling pieces, and any other weapons they could scrape together. He also managed to obtain the help of 18 soldiers and 10 cavalrymen.

At midnight the mob converged on the bank from the twisted alleys of Cheapside, the broad King William Street, and the narrow lane of Threadneedle Street. As they rushed towards the bank, they found themselves confronted by Wilkes and his little band of troops and militiamen.

As soon as Wilkes was recognized, a great shout of delight went up from the mob. There were happy cries of "45!", "Wilkes and Liberty!" and "No Popery." No one supposed for a minute that Wilkes would interfere with them. Wilkes held up his hand for silence.

"My friends, the bank cannot be destroyed!" he shouted. "You have done enough for the Protestant cause. Go home to your families."

A furious shout went up. There were the usual cries of "Papist!" "Romanist!" and several voices shouted, "Do you defend Catholics?"

Wilkes quietly replied, "I believe that anyone, even an atheist, has the right to fair treatment."

Politics make strange bedfellows and the circle had come full round. The atheist Wilkes who had spent a large part of his life ridiculing the Catholic Church was now defending it. Perhaps he felt that if the mob were allowed to deny Catholics the right of freedom of thought, they might next turn on atheists, which would be an outrageous state of affairs.

The raging crowd charged the bank, and Wilkes gave

the fatal order to fire. The muskets crashed out in a volley and the mob fell back, leaving their dead and dying on the cobblestones.

Seven times the mob charged the bank, led by an unidentified young man riding a white horse, who kept shouting "Down with the Pope!" Each time they were met by the deliberate fire of the militia. Finally they staggered away, first by twos and threes and then in large groups. The bank and Great Britain had been saved.

Now that Wilkes had dared to show that the mob could be beaten back, the Lord Mayor plucked up courage enough to call out the troops. Cavalry and infantry swept through the gutted city and restored order. Horace Walpole saw a company of the Horse Guards returning with their bayonets dripping blood. Two hundred eighty-five people were killed in the fighting. Twenty-nine were hanged later. How many died in the fires, drank themselves to death, or were killed by the looters no one knows.

Lord George was brought to trial but was acquitted of any responsibility in the riots, partly because he was the son of a duke and partly because the jury honestly believed that he had no real knowledge of what he was doing. The great defender of the Protestant cause then announced that he had become converted to Judaism. He insisted on being circumcised (the operation was performed so crudely that he nearly died as a result). He grew a long beard, and went about in a long cloak, wearing a flat, broad-brimmed hat.

He gave big dinner parties for his friends while wearing this getup, and the contrast between this weird figure and the elegant exquisites and the elaborately gowned ladies must have been very interesting. He then launched a wild attack on the Queen of France, which got the government into a diplomatic tangle and finally caused him to be sent to Newgate Prison. He died there in 1793. His last moments were greatly embittered because the Jews refused to allow him to be buried in a Jewish graveyard. They took the attitude that he wasn't a real convert—just crazy.

Wilkes was ruined, as he knew he would be. The mob never forgave him and he was left without supporters. However, he promptly turned his coat and became one of the King's most ardent backers. Quite a comedown for the man who had singlehandedly defied not only the monarchy but also Parliament. Still, Wilkes had not much choice. The people had let him down in the Gordon riots and he had to make a living.

Wilkes' sudden turnabout from being a violent independent to a cringing sycophant of royalty caused a lot of humorous remarks. At a state reception, the futile Prince of Wales, who had often been the butt of Wilkes' sarcasm, turned to the discredited statesman and spitefully quoted a jingle that Sheridan had written:

"Johnny Wilkes, Johnny Wilkes,
Thou greatest of bilks,

How changed are the notes you now sing;
Your famed Forty-five
Is Prerogative,
And your blasphemy 'God Save the King'."

Wilkes still had a few kicks left in him and he paid his royal tormentor back at a dinner a few days later. Wilkes proposed a toast to the King. "Long life to His Majesty," Wilkes announced, adding, "And I am sure his Royal Highness, the Prince of Wales, will join me in drinking this toast."

As it was well known that the Prince hated his father and was counting the days until he could become king, this toast put him in a spot. He couldn't very well refuse to drink to the King's health but the Prince angrily blurted out, "Since when did you become so solicitous of the King's health, John Wilkes?"

With a low bow Wilkes replied, "Ever since I first had the honor of knowing your Royal Highness."

Wilkes was able to joke about his fall. Once he was asked to take part in a card game. He refused, saying, "My eyesight is now so bad that I can't tell a king from a knave."

Perhaps Wilkes' switch of loyalties wasn't completely a matter of opportunism. He may have felt that after the riots the country needed a king and a strong upper class—even a man like George III and an upper class composed of rakes. There had to be some force to control the mob.

Wilkes continued to hold various minor governmental jobs with the strict understanding that he would use whatever little influence he had left to support the King's policies. But the government no longer had anything to fear from him. As Wilkes himself remarked, "I have become an extinct volcano." He lived on the Isle of Wight, collecting Wedgwood china and translating Latin poets. He also kept up a voluminous correspondence with his numerous lady friends. He died on Christmas day, 1797.

Unlike most men of his time, Wilkes, as has been mentioned, had always been very generous to his bastard children and had even supported the illegitimate son and daughter of Charles Churchill. He had an illegitimate daughter named Harriet, the daughter of a lady he'd met one day at Bath, whom he finally married off to a worthy young man, and an illegitimate son called Jack Smith by his housekeeper. Wilkes paid for Jack's commission as an officer in the Hessian guards but made him promise never to fight against the Americans. His favorite child was always his legitimate daughter, Polly. Polly stayed with him until the end and father and daughter were devoted to each other. Polly died a few years afterward. She never married.

In his will, Wilkes left generous sums not only to Polly but also to his other children and even to his various mistresses. But when the will came to be probated, it was discovered that Wilkes was not only broke but heavily in debt. He died as he had lived—penniless but cheerful.

Wilkes asked that he be buried in the South Audley Church in London and that the pallbearers be six poor men chosen from the London mob. The request was granted. On his gravestone was inscribed: "The remains of John Wilkes, the Friend of Liberty."

Wilkes was one of the last of the Hell-Fire Club to go. Among the first had been Thomas Potter, the spendthrift son of the archbishop of Canterbury, who died in 1759 at the age of forty. Charles Churchill had died at 33 in France during his self-imposed exile with Wilkes. Churchill's devoted friend and follower, Robert Lloyd, the young poet, died in a debtor's prison apparently of a broken heart at the age of 32 after hearing of Churchill's death. Bubb-Dodington developed dropsy and put himself in the hands of a quack who tortured him with fake cures. He finally fell downstairs in a fit and died in 1762.

Paul Whitehead, the club's secretary, collapsed after the death of his imbecile wife. He died in 1774. A lifelong atheist (or Satanist), he had always refused to go near a church but he willed his heart to Dashwood together with 50 pounds for the purchase of a marble urn to hold it. He requested that the urn be placed in a great mausoleum over the caves which Dashwood had built for members of his family and a few intimate friends. Dashwood turned out the Bucks Militia for the ceremony. The urn was carried in state around West Wycombe Park and then three times around the mausoleum before it was placed in a niche to the music of a fife and drum corps. The heart became a tourist attraction and was regularly shown to visitors for a small fee. It soon shriveled and turned black and the guide always explained that Whitehead's heart "was as black in death as it had been in life." The heart was stolen by a souvenir hunter in 1839.

The public never forgave Sandwich for his attack on Wilkes' *Essay on Woman. The Beggar's Opera* was playing in London at the time and one of the characters in the play, telling of a notorious scoundrel who had betrayed his best friend to the authorities, remarks, "Well, I never expected to hear that Jemmy Twitcher had peached!" This remark brought down the house and Sandwich was ever afterwards known as "Jemmy Twitcher." He was later made head of the University of Cambridge, but the students left the dining hall when he entered the room.

In his old age, Sandwich acquired a young girl called Martha Ray as his mistress. The old rake seems genuinely to have loved the girl and appeared everywhere with her. A young curate also fell in love with Miss Ray and offered her honorable matrimony but the girl preferred a life of guilty splendor. One evening while Sandwich and Martha were entering his carriage, the curate rushed up, put a pistol to Miss Ray's head, and shot her dead. He then tried to kill himself with another pistol but the bullet missed his brain. He was later hanged for the murder of Miss Ray.

Curiously, none of Sandwich's other crimes aroused so much public resentment as this affair. It was claimed that he had prevented the girl from marrying and driven the curate mad with his brutality. Sandwich was forced to leave society and retired to semiseclusion in the country. He died in 1792. It was suggested having inscribed on his tombstone, "Seldom has any man held so many offices and accomplished so little," but this idea was never carried out.

After denouncing the government for its pusillanimous attitude toward the American Colonists and for trying to prevent the repeal of the Stamp Act, Lord Bute retired from politics an embittered man. He spent most of his declining years in Italy, determined, as he said, "to retire from the world before it retires from me." He died in 1792.

The remarkable Chevalier D'Eon remained in London, but as he had become worthless as a political agent he lost the support of Louis XV. The Chevalier was left penniless and finally blackmailed the French King by threatening to publish Louis' letters to him. The publication of these letters would have proven most embarrassing to Louis as they showed plainly that he had spent thousand of livres in an attempt to undermine the British government and had subsidized Wilkes and other agitators. Finally a deal was worked out between the Chevalier and the French government by which d'Eon surrendered the letters in return for a yearly income of 12,000 livres but agreed to announce that he was definitely a woman and always to wear woman's clothes. As it was then considered impossible for any government to employ a woman for important diplomatic undercover work, the Chevalier's announcement definitely precluded any suspicion of his real mission in England. However, the official reason given for the King's demand was to "eliminate bets, lawsuits, and duels."

The Chevalier agreed and from then on was known as the Chevalier d'Eon. He always dressed as a woman but refused to give up his great hobby of fencing. He used to take on all comers at Angelo's famous fencing salon, fencing away in a huge hoop-skirt and wearing a large wig. It became generally accepted that he was a woman although as Walpole remarked, "The lady's hands always seemed fitter to carry a chair than wave a fan."

The Chevalier died in 1810. The priest who had attended him until the end lifted up the sheet and then staggered back with the cry, "It's a man!" The secret of the Chevalier's sex had at last been solved.

Sir Francis Dashwood, the founder and guiding spirit of the club, became too old for orgies. He lived the life of a quiet, retired English gentleman on his great estate at West

Wycombe. He was fond of reminiscing about the good old days in the abbey and the caves, but there were few people left who could remember when the courts of Europe had trembled when the Hell-Fire Club held a meeting. His most intimate friend had been Paul Whitehead, and Sir Francis deeply mourned his loss. He developed the habit of taking walks during the long English evenings in his vast gardens, alone with his memories.

After one such walk, he staggered into his mansion deathly white and collapsed on the floor. "I saw Paul White-head among the yews!" he gasped. "He beckoned to me!" The Lord le Despencer took to his bed and never left it. He died a few days later on December 11, 1781.

So passed the greatest of this strange company of men who for a few short years held the destiny of the world in their hands and dissipated their extraordinary talents which might have held America for the British Empire . . . brilliant and resourceful they were, but immoral and futile.

EPILOGUE: A SENTIMENTAL JOURNEY

(Affectionately dedicated to the memory of Laurence
Sterne, member of the Hell-Fire Club 1745–1768)

While I was in England in 1958, I decided to make a pil-
grimage to the various shrines connected with the Hell-Fire
Club and pour a little "divine milk punch" on the grave of
Sir Francis.

I went first to the inn that saw the beginnings of the
Hell-Fire Club in 1746 . . . the George and Vulture which still
stands in George Yard, not far from the Bank of England
and up a series of alleys that twist like a snake with colic
. . . Castle Court, St. Michael's Alley, Bell Yard, and Change
Alley. I passed men carrying stacks of yard-long loaves of
bread in great baskets, hurrying men in high hats (professional messengers) and whistling boys in white aprons who
threaded their way through the maze of alleys with the sure-

ness of long practice. I passed the four tall towers of old St. Michael's Church, a small rectory garden hidden away among the tangle of buildings, part of the old Roman wall 2,000 years old, and finally came to George Yard.

The inn looks much as it always has . . . open fires over which steaks, chops, and roasts are cooked and a plentiful supply of ales, beers, and wines. Under my feet was the cellar where Sir Francis, Whitehead, Churchill, Potter, and the other founding members first celebrated the ritual of the Black Mass.

Today the George and the Vulture is famous as being the inn so frequently mentioned in Dickens' *Pickwick Papers*. Dickens himself often stayed here and his room is preserved as a memorial. The present-day Pickwick Club, a group of Dickens enthusiasts, hold their meetings in this room.

The proprietor was only too happy to show me around. I saw the yard where Mr. Pickwick supposedly hired Sam Weller; the ladle with which Dickens stirred his punch; the picture of Dickens over the clock in the entrance hall, a statue of Mr. Pickwick on the steps; and the table on which Dickens wrote some of his novels.

"Where's the table where the Hell-Fire Club laid the naked girls to celebrate the Black Mass?" I wanted to know.

The proprietor froze. "Sir, we do not refer to the inn's connection with that organization. Now if you will follow me I will show you our collection of Dickens' prints."

I didn't bother to see the prints. I did, however, order a bottle of claret and drank to the memory of "Hell Fire" Francis wherever he may be.

I tried to see the ruins of the abbey of Medmenham but this proved to be impossible. I was told at the British Museum that even by 1764 the abbey had become a real ruin. The roofs had fallen in and boys had smashed all the pornographic statuary. It passed through several hands, the owners charging admission to see the "haunted house." Then, at the request of the clergy, the "Black Chapel" with its indecent paintings was torn down. As the chapel was the main tourist attraction, the abbey afterwards ceased to "draw" and was abandoned. Today, the abbey—or what is left of it—is owned by a gentleman who has a positive rule that no sightseers are to be allowed anywhere on the grounds. Recently I was told that the land has been sold and a housing development has been built on the site, although whether or not this is true I haven't been able to find out.

Next I took a train to High Wycombe and from there a bus to West Wycombe to see the famous caves and West Wycombe Park. The village of West Wycombe has been preserved by the government as one of the oldest and most picturesque communities in England. No modern buildings can be put up and no factories are permitted. There are still the thatched cottages, old inns with their signs swinging in the wind, and half-framed buildings, exactly as the town must have appeared in Sir Francis' day. The little Wye still runs past the village, scarcely ten feet across at its widest part.

I followed a broad gravel road through a magnificent woods to the mansion. There in the midst of lawns as finely clipped as a putting green stood the famous home built by "Hell-Fire" Francis. There was the great North Front overlooking the park and lake with its Ionic columns said to be the finest example of the Palladian style in England. I walked around by the Temple of Bacchus (still intact), and having paid my two shillings joined a guided tour of the mansion. The garden and grounds are now owned by the National Trust, a governmental institution organized to preserve some of the great relics of England's past. The guide was a young man employed by the government to show tourists around. That day I was the only tourist except for two small boys.

We went through the Passage Hall covered with faded marble paper into an open loggia. Then we had to enter the house a second time through a door which opened into the Staircase Hall. This curious arrangement was devised by Sir Francis to give his visitors a sense of mystery. The Staircase Hall has at either end a screen of fluted Ionic columns. On the walls are huge paintings of the "Creation of Eve" and "The Fall" either by Borgnis or Hannan. The Chippendale mahogany staircase with its inlays of box and yew woods is still polished and undamaged.

I followed the guide to the Tapestry Room, The Dining-Room, the Brown Drawing-Room, the Blue Drawing-Room, the Music Salon, the Library and the Gallery. I saw a painting of Sir Francis in his monk's costume holding up a chalice to the goddess Venus and blessing her with the other hand. I saw a marble bust of Paul Whitehead and the original "Franklin-Despencer" prayer book. I saw the enormous ceiling paintings of mythological scenes by Borgnis and Hannan and the crumbling Mereworth tapestries.

The two boys would occasionally correct the guide on some point. Finally he asked irritably, "How do you nippers know so much about it?" "Oh, we live here," the kids replied cheerfully. "We have a flat on the second floor but we've never been downstairs before."

Later, the guide explained to me that to help pay the cost of preserving the gigantic mansion, the second floor has been divided into apartments and rented. "But the present baronet is allowed to live here in a small suite of rooms," he added.

I wandered by myself through the park. The Swan Lake is still there and the Temple of Music continues to stand on its tiny island. The gardens have completely gone. They required so many gardeners to keep them up that the National Trust couldn't afford it. Nothing remains of the curious temple shaped "like the door by which we all entered the world" or the pillar that so frightened young girls when they came on it unexpectedly. In 1800, Sir Francis' descendants hired Humphrey Repton, the great landscapist, to make "judicious alterations," and the temple, the pillar, and the famous garden shaped like a naked woman were the first items to go. The suggestive statuary was also destroyed.

I strolled along paths where Wilkes had ridden down posthaste from London to report that the betting on the sex of the Chevalier d'Eon was running 7 to 5 that he was a woman; where Franklin and Sir Francis had walked while arguing over the correct wording of the Book of Common Prayer; where Kitty Fisher (who inspired the nursery rhyme "Lucy Locket lost her pocket, Kitty Fisher found it," after Lord Sandwich switched mistresses) once swished the famous hoop-skirts under which Lord Mountford had tried to hide.

I left West Wycombe Park, crossed the village, and climbed the hill on which St. Lawrence's church still stands. It was easy to find, for from the park I had been able to see the great golden ball on top where Dashwood and Wilkes drank their "divine milk punch." Over the church door is inscribed "Memento." The usual inscription over church doors is "Memento Mori" (remember death) but Dashwood had put up "Memento Meri" (remember drinking). The last word was later erased.

Inside, the church glowed in a curious red light filtered through the stained glass windows. I saw on a marble tablet in the chancel "The Blood Hand," a remarkable reddish stain suggesting an outspread hand, which appeared shortly after Sir Francis' death. No one has ever been able to wash it off. I climbed the 100-foot tower to the Golden Ball. The iron ladder is still there by which the friars entered the ball, but the ball is kept locked nowadays. Fanatics made several attempts to burn down the church after Sir Francis' death— one man piling up all the hymnals and setting fire to them. The church is maintained entirely by the village, although "It's on top of the hill and they're on the bottom." It was suggested that part of the revenue that comes from taking visitors through the caves be given to the church, but the minister turned down the idea. Like Sandwich, the caves "can never lose the smell of brimstone."

Below the church is the Mausoleum, a huge structure and most impressive. It is an oval perhaps a hundred feet across with walls some thirty feet high, open at the top. Inside, set into the wall, are niches for the bodies of the Dashwood family and friends. There are dozens of busts but nearly all have been mutilated in some way or other and many are reproductions of the originals. After Dashwood's death, the Mausoleum was frequently attacked by righteous individuals eager to show their hatred of the notorious Hell-Fire monks. Sir Francis himself is buried in a vault in the church.

Below the church and the Mausoleum are the caves.

These are still owned by the Dashwood family and are kept as a tourist attraction. There is a booth by the entrance where drinks and souvenirs are sold. I saw "Divine Milk Punch" advertised and ordered a glass. The damn stuff *was* milk.

"I know, sir," said the counterman apologetically. "But we don't have a liquor license."

The caves are still quite eerie. You must have a guide, otherwise you'd quickly become lost. An occasional bat whisks by overhead. A low mist rises from the floor. I saw the carved devils' heads on the walls, the cursing well where the High Priestess was baptized, the entrance to the secret passage leading to the church and the River Styx. The river is now only a small stream. Because bits of chalk were continually falling from the roof of the Banqueting Hall, workmen were hired to dig a passage around the room. In so doing they apparently changed the course of the underground river for the floor of the Banqueting Hall is now under a couple of inches of water.

After the tour was over, I remarked cheerfully to the guide, "Well, the only thing left for me to see is Sir Francis Dashwood."

"Certainly, sir," replied the guide calmly. "He's in the Robing Room getting ready for the evening ceremony but he'll be along in a few minutes."

This I had to see. I sat down to wait. A little while later, a brisk, business-like man hurried out of the caves.

"This gentleman is waiting to see you, sir," called the guide.

It turned out that this was Sir John Dashwood, the present baronet. As Sir Francis left no legitimate children, the title and the estate passed to his half-brother. Sir John is the tenth baronet to live at West Wycombe.

Sir John is an energetic, business-like man whose main source of income now comes from the caves. He told me that he was hoping to introduce new lighting effects to give the caverns an even more ghostly atmosphere. "I'm now working on an idea for a pageant," he explained. "Actors in monks' robes and girls playing the part of nuns. Should be quite impressive. Too bad my proper Victorian ancestors destroyed all Sir Francis' statuary, temples and so on. They'd be worth quite a packet to me now."

"Aren't you embarrassed at being the descendant of such a notorious man as Sir Francis?"

"Certainly not," said Sir John briskly. From the entrance to the cave we could see West Wycombe and the Park. Sir John stood looking at the lands which had belonged to his family for over 200 years. "By God, if I'd only had a few more ancestors who showed as much imagination as old Francis, I wouldn't have had to turn the estate over to that bloody National Trust."

AN OPEN LETTER TO OUR VALUED READERS

What do Raymond Chandler, Arthur C. Clarke, Isaac Asimov, Irving Wallace, Ben Bova, Stuart Kaminsky and over a dozen other authors have in common? They are all part of an exciting new line of **ibooks** distributed by Simon and Schuster.

 ibooks represent the best of the future and the best of the past...a voyage into the future of books that unites traditional printed books with the excitement of the web.

Please join us in developing the first new publishing imprint of the 21st century.

We're planning terrific offers for ibooks readers...virtual reading groups where you can chat online about ibooks authors...message boards where you can communicate with fellow readers...downloadable free chapters of ibooks for your reading pleasure...free readers services such as a directory of where to find electronic books on the web...special discounts on books and other items of interest to readers...

The evolution of the book is www.ibooksinc.com.